Cambridge Elements ⁼

Elements in Publishing and Book Culture
edited by
Samantha Rayner
University College London
Leah Tether
University of Bristol

BLUESTOCKINGS AND TRAVEL ACCOUNTS

Reading, Writing and Collecting

Nataliia Voloshkova
Dragomanov National Pedagogical University

CAMBRIDGE
UNIVERSITY PRESS

CAMBRIDGE
UNIVERSITY PRESS

University Printing House, Cambridge CB2 8BS, United Kingdom

One Liberty Plaza, 20th Floor, New York, NY 10006, USA

477 Williamstown Road, Port Melbourne, VIC 3207, Australia

314–321, 3rd Floor, Plot 3, Splendor Forum, Jasola District Centre,
New Delhi – 110025, India

79 Anson Road, #06–04/06, Singapore 079906

Cambridge University Press is part of the University of Cambridge.

It furthers the University's mission by disseminating knowledge in the pursuit of
education, learning, and research at the highest international levels of excellence.

www.cambridge.org
Information on this title: www.cambridge.org/9781108720724
DOI: 10.1017/9781108767514

© Nataliia Voloshkova 2021

First published 2021

A catalogue record for this publication is available from the British Library.

ISBN 978-1-108-72072-4 Paperback
ISSN 2514-8524 (online)
ISSN 2514-8516 (print)

Bluestockings and Travel Accounts

Reading, Writing and Collecting

Elements in Publishing and Book Culture

DOI: 10.1017/9781108767514

First published online: January 2021

Nataliia Voloshkova

Dragomanov National Pedagogical University

Author for correspondence: Nataliia Voloshkova, natavoloshkova@yahoo.com

ABSTRACT: This Element proposes to relate the eighteenth-century world of travel and travel writing with the Bluestocking salon. It locates eminent British travellers and explorers in the female-presided intellectual space and examines their multifaceted interaction with the Bluestockings between 1760 and 1799. The study shows how the Bluestockings acquired knowledge of the world through reading, discussing, writing and collecting travel accounts. It explores the 'social life' of manuscripts and printed travel texts in the circle, their popularity and impact on the Bluestockings. This Element builds upon the body of evidence provided by their published and unpublished diaries, correspondence and private library catalogues.

KEYWORDS: bluestockings and reading, eighteenth-century travellers, reading practices, women's book ownership, women's travel writing

ISBNs: 9781108720724 (PB), 9781108767514 (OC)

ISSNs: 2514-8524 (online), 2514-8516 (print)

Contents

1 Introduction

The eighteenth century saw a phenomenal rise in the popularity of travel accounts which continued well into the nineteenth century. Numerous scholars, explorers and travellers chose to document their explorations, travel observations and experiences either in print or in manuscript. These works were never short of eager readers. Most travelogues in the period did not relate travels in the proper sense of the word. In the time when many academic disciplines were still in the process of formation and boundaries between them, as well as differences between 'professional' and 'amateur' scholars, were blurred and indistinct, non-fiction travel accounts frequently presented narratives in which details of travel itineraries and/or residence particulars were incorporated into the body of scholarly texts on history, ethnography, natural history or art of a specific region or country. The contents of travelogues depended largely on the author's educational background, intellectual interests or scholarly pursuits, target reading audience and the purpose of sharing his or her travel report and making 'public' the knowledge acquired during travels.

Recent decades have seen ever-increasing scholarly attention to travel writing. This study is following in Jan Borm's footsteps; he defines the travel book as 'any narrative characterized by a non-fiction dominant that relates (almost always) in the first person a journey or journeys that the reader supposes to have taken place in reality while assuming or presupposing that author, narrator and principal character are but one identical'.[1] Recent research has offered novel critical approaches to travelogues, explored narrative techniques and brought to the forefront the ideas behind them. Forgotten manuscripts have been uncovered and many well-known travelogues have been reread. Scholars have focused on women's travel writing; their recent findings 'greatly nuanced our understanding of women's contribution to the genre'.[2] Although extensive research on

---

[1] J. Borm, 'Defining Travel: On the Travel Book, Travel Writing and Terminology' in G. Hooper and T. Youngs (eds.), *Perspectives on Travel Writing* (Aldershot: Ashgate, 2004), p. 17.

[2] C. Thompson, 'Journeys to Authority: Reassessing Women's Early Travel Writing, 1763–1862', *Women's Writing*, 24.2 (2017), 131.

eighteenth-century travel writers and their works has been carried out, female recipients of travelogues have been under-examined in critical studies.[3] In this light, the recovering of the reading, discussing, writing and collecting of travel accounts by a group of women can add to a collective portrait of eighteenth-century readers and, consequently, contribute to a more coherent understanding of the travel-writing phenomenon in the period. It can also diversify our understanding of a cultural landscape of female reading and book ownership and circulation.

This Element narrows the focus and explores the 'social life' of travel accounts and 'social circulation' of geographical knowledge in the Bluestocking circle between 1760 and 1799, the period when many travelogues were 'at the forefront of scientific and intellectual inquiry'.[4] It discusses the popularity, significance and impact of the travel book on the Bluestockings, women whose 'public personae were built around intellectual accomplishment (as reflected in textual production), female friendship, Anglican centred piety, and social responsibility.'[5] This study offers to expand the circle by including less known Mary Hamilton (1756–1816),

---

[3] A few publications touch on the problem: Z. Kinsley, *Women Writing the Home Tour, 1682–1812* (Bodmin: Ashgate, 2008); J. Pearson, *Women's Reading in Britain, 1750–1830: A Dangerous Recreation* (New York: Cambridge University Press, 1999); B. Hagglund, *Tourists and Travellers: Women's Non-fictional Writing about Scotland, 1770–1830* (Bristol: Channel View Publications, 2010); D. Allan, *Commonplace Books and Reading in Georgian England* (Cambridge: Cambridge University Press, 2010); M. Towsey, '"I can't resist sending you the book": Private Libraries, Elite Women, and Shared Reading Practices in Georgian Britain', *Library & Information History*, 29.3 (2013), 210–22.

[4] C. Thompson, *Travel Writing* (London and New York: Routledge, 2011), p. 33.

[5] B.A. Schellenberg, 'Bluestocking Women and the Negotiation of Oral, Manuscript, and Print Cultures' in J.M. Labbe (ed.), *The History of British Women's Writing, 1750–1830* (Chippenham and Eastbourne: Palgrave Macmillan, 2010), pp. 64–5. The terms 'Bluestocking' and 'bluestocking' as well as the composition of the circle have been the subject of scholarly discussion. See, for example, E. Major, *Madam Britannia: Women, Church, and Nation, 1712–1812* (New York: Oxford University Press, 2012), pp. 81–4.

Eva Maria Garrick (1724–1822), Charlotte Walsingham (1738–90) and Lady Catherine Herries (c.1753–1808), who, like the celebrated first- and second-generation Bluestockings, were well-known society figures in London in the 1780s.[6] These accomplished women attended and hosted conversation parties in their London homes, engaged in philanthropic and patronage activities and were constantly 'in the pursuit of intellectual improvement' and 'polite sociability'.[7] A number of recent publications have shown that the Bluestockings were prolific readers, though their reading of travel books has not been considered in detail to date.[8] This study addresses such topics as the Bluestockings' interaction with travel- lers and explorers, reading practices related to travel accounts, discussion and critical judgement of travelogues as well as production of journals and letters during travels. The Element also looks at three book collections owned by these accomplished women and shows a significant number of travelogue titles, geography books and printed materials related to geo- graphy in them. In doing this, an attempt is made to explore the ways in which knowledge about the world was acquired, accumulated and diffused by the Bluestockings and to demonstrate that the intellectual female reader

---

[6] Evidence of social engagement and activities of these four women whom I regard as members of the group of younger Bluestockings can be gleaned from the Bluestockings' correspondence, diaries and memoirs. Regretfully, Garrick, Walsingham and Herries still remain 'in shadow' and are waiting for their researchers.

[7] N. Pohl and B.A. Schellenberg, 'Introduction: A Bluestocking Historiography' in N. Pohl and B.A. Schellenberg (eds.), *Reconsidering the Bluestockings* (San Marino, CA: Huntington Library, 2003), p. 2.

[8] C. Lupton, *Reading and the Making of Time in the Eighteenth Century* (Baltimore: Johns Hopkins University Press, 2018); M. Ellis, 'Reading Practices in Elizabeth Montagu's Epistolary Network of the 1750' in E. Eger (ed.), *Bluestockings Displayed: Portraiture, Performance and Patronage, 1730–1830* (New York: Cambridge University Press, 2013), pp. 213–32; B.A. Schellenberg, 'Reading in an Epistolary Community in Eighteenth-Century England' in D.R. Sedo (ed.), *Reading Communities from Salons to Cyberspace* (Chippenham and Eastbourne: Palgrave Macmillan, 2011), pp. 25–43.

constituted an indispensable part of the success which travelogues enjoyed in Britain in the second half of the eighteenth century.

The present study lies at the intersection of three rapidly developing research areas – studies in travel writing, the history of reading and Bluestocking studies and the seminal works in these areas.[9] It is largely based on evidence from primary sources – numerous records found in unpublished and published diaries; travel journals and correspondence of the Bluestockings; and, above all, on their records related to the reading and discussing of travel accounts. Comments of this kind are not rare in eighteenth-century private papers; however, in most cases, they are laconic, cursory and scattered here and there. Such records, although they provide important insights into many aspects related to the travel writing of the day, have been underexplored until now. Traditionally, they have performed a supportive function in critical literature and have occasionally been used to illustrate the response of the reading audience. The Bluestockings' records of the reading and discussing of travel accounts are the cornerstones on which the key arguments of this study rest. The study also uses evidence from memoirs and correspondence of the literary men and travellers who were closely associated with the Bluestockings.

The Element also rests on information provided by three sales catalogues of the Bluestockings' private book collections and a manuscript inventory. According to John Brewer, catalogues as a primary source have been under-examined until now, as researchers frequently experience difficulty in animating such 'inert sources'.[10] The

---

[9] Pohl and Schellenberg (eds.), *Reconsidering the Bluestockings*; E. Eger, *Bluestockings: Women of Reason from Enlightenment to Romanticism* (Chippenham and Eastbourne: Palgrave Macmillan, 2010) and D. Heller (ed.), *Bluestockings Now! The Evolution of a Social Role* (Farnham: Ashgate, 2015) on the Bluestockings; Thompson, *Travel Writing* on travel writing; A. Williams, *The Social Life of Books: Reading Together in the Eighteenth-Century Home* (New Haven and London: Yale University Press, 2017) on the history of reading.

[10] J. Brewer, 'Reconstructing the Reader: Prescriptions, Texts and Strategies on Anna Larpent's Reading' in J. Raven, H. Small and N. Tadmor (eds.), *The Practice and Representation of Reading in England* (Cambridge: Cambridge University Press, 1996), p. 227.

present study attempts to 'animate' them by providing information on both the library owners and their Bluestocking friends who had access to the collections and borrowed books from them. The Element establishes the links between these groups of primary sources which complement each other. By interpreting, comparing and analysing the extensive evidence, it attempts to give an idea of how travel accounts were read, discussed, written and collected in the Bluestocking circle. In doing this, the study seeks to deepen our understanding of the role which the Bluestockings played in cultural production and knowledge diffusion of the period.

The material presented in the book is organised in four thematically entitled sections. Section 2, *Bluestockings, Travellers and Conversation*, looks at the Bluestocking drawing room as a space for learned conversations on travel and exploration in which contemporary geographers, explorers and travellers obtained an opportunity for face-to-face contact with the 'women of independence and confidence, who intervened influentially in the major cultural debates of their times'.[11] This section traces the Bluestockings' connections with the most eminent travel writers and explorers of the day. It argues that their interaction was mutually beneficial as 'learning, knowledge creation, and innovation are all fruit of the circulation and interpretation of information, the co-creation of new ideas, cumulative experience, and cognition'.[12] Their interaction encompassed a range of interlinked practices which included the discussing of oral travel reports and printed travel accounts, collective viewing of drawings and prints and examining samples and specimens brought from travels. An attempt is made to reveal the Bluestockings' instrumentality in geographical knowledge diffusion, organisation of scientific trips and promotion of travelogue publishing projects.

Section 3, *Reading Travelogues*, aims to reconstruct the reading of 'travels and voyages' in the Bluestocking circle between 1760 and 1799,

[11] Eger, *Bluestockings*, p. 20.

[12] J. Glückler, E. Lazega and I. Hammer, 'Exploring the Interaction of Space and Networks in the Creation of Knowledge: An Introduction' in J. Glückler, E. Lazega and I. Hammer (eds.), *Knowledge and Networks* (Springer Open), p. 4.

focusing particularly on the 1780s. The findings presented in this and other sections of the Element are heavily based upon the evidence found in two linked manuscript collections. These are the Mary Hamilton papers and the Dickenson Family of Birch Hall Papers;[13] the material from them has been partially published to date.[14] Mary Hamilton was a voracious reader who documented her reading habits and interests in much detail. Hamilton's diaries reveal how she enjoyed London's cultivated atmosphere in the 1780s and befriended a host of celebrated literary women and men of the late Georgian period.[15] More evidence comes from the published letters and diaries of the Bluestockings – Elizabeth Carter, Elizabeth Montagu, Frances Boscawen, Hannah More, Frances Burney, Mary Delany, Hester Lynch Thrale Piozzi (hereafter referred to as Thrale Piozzi), Hester Chapone, Catherine Talbot – and the literary men Horace Walpole and William Weller Pepys who were closely associated with the Bluestocking circle.

Section 3 attempts to explore how these accomplished women chose and read travel accounts and the ways in which they accessed them. It also reveals the highly popular titles of the genre read by these sophisticated females and their expectations of solid travel books. The section argues that notwithstanding a variety of travelogues published in Britain, their reading was not unsystematic and random but selective and accentuated. The evidence presented in the section and Appendix 1 gives an idea of the scope of travel books read by the Bluestockings and suggests that the most recent travelogues were always on their radar; information on them spread either by word of mouth or via correspondence. This section attempts to

---

[13] Mary Hamilton Papers. University of Manchester Library. GB 133 HAM/ (cited subsequently as HAM/); Dickenson Family of Birch Hall. Preston, Lancashire Archives. DDX 274 (cited subsequently as DDX/).

[14] Excerpts from Hamilton's diaries and correspondence appear in E. Anson and F. Anson (eds.), *Mary Hamilton, afterwards Mrs. John Dickenson, at Court and at Home, from Letters and Diaries, 1756 to 1816* (London: John Murray, 1925) and L. Llanover (ed.), *The Autobiography and Correspondence of Mary Granville, Mrs. Delany*, 3 vols. (London: Richard Bentley, 1862).

[15] For more information on Hamilton's life, see N. Voloshkova, '"My friend Mr. H. Walpole": Mary Hamilton, Horace Walpole and the Art of Conversation', *Image [&] Narrative*, 18.3 (2017), 96–7.

identify the core travelogues which were widely read and discussed in the Bluestocking circle between 1780 and 1790 and to explain the motives behind their popularity. It also discusses a group of women-authored travelogues read by the Bluestockings and suggests that the choice of travel books depended on their interest in a certain country rather than on the author's gender. Section 3 discusses the Bluestockings' reading habits. As printed travel accounts were 'central to the canon of respectable, desirable reading'[16] in the eighteenth century, it also traces how these women cultivated knowledge of geography and love for reading travels in their children and relations.

Section 4, *Writing Travel Accounts*, seeks to show that the Bluestockings were not only well informed and sophisticated readers of journeys but also well-travelled women of the day. Like many eighteenth-century men, they recorded their travels in the country and continental Europe. This section focuses on the Bluestockings' activity in producing travel accounts and explores their 'social' life. It analyses the evidence from their diaries and correspondence that bespeaks the ongoing circulation of travel texts in manuscript and the value which their recipients ascribed to them. By way of illustration, it shows how Carter's continental letters to Talbot found a response in the addressee's family and acquaintants and how three letters on journeying the Lake District were copied and read out by Hamilton. It is suggested that through writing travel texts, the Bluestockings not only improved their literary style and indirectly encouraged their readers to adopt similar writing practices. They also participated in cultural production and knowledge diffusion in the period. This section points out that Thrale Piozzi was the most ardent and prolific writer of manuscript travel journals in the Bluestocking circle; after the publication of her travelogue, she entered a group of very few female travel writers in eighteenth-century Britain.

Section 5, *Collecting Travel Books*, continues to explore the Bluestockings' engagement with travel books, focusing on three private collections possessed by Elizabeth Vesey, Eva Maria Garrick and Thrale Piozzi. It reveals a considerable number of travelogues as well as geography

---

[16] Thompson, *Travel Writing*, pp. 33–4.

books and printed materials related to geography in their libraries; further details on the relevant book titles, which have been identified in the printed saleroom catalogues and Thrale Piozzi's manuscript book inventory, are given in Appendices 2, 3, 4 and 5. This section suggests that the Bluestockings were active consumers of travel accounts; the ownership of travelogues, other books and materials on geography bespeaks not only their fascination with travel accounts but also serves as important evidence for the ongoing acquisition, diffusion and production of geographical knowledge in the Bluestocking circle. The section also seeks to contribute to our knowledge of eighteenth-century book collections owned by women as the 'role of private libraries in the history of reading is rather more hidden from view – particularly in Britain.'[17]

---

[17] Towsey, ' "I can't resist sending you the book," ' p. 211.

2 Bluestockings, Travellers and Conversation

> Hail, Conversation, heav'nly fair,
> Thou bliss of life, and balm of care!
> Call forth the long-forgotten knowledge
> Of school, of travel, and of college![18]

Praising Elizabeth Carter's diligent studies of ancient languages and philosophy, the editor of her correspondence, Montagu Pennington, informed readers about the lack of his aunt's interest in contemporary travels by noting that the Bluestocking 'took great delight in ancient geography'; with it, 'she was much more conversant than with modern geography . . . of which she had only a general, and, in some cases, merely a superficial knowledge.'[19] According to Pennington, the renowned translator of Epictetus 'could give a better account of the wanderings of Ulysses and Aeneas, than she could of the voyages and discoveries of Cook and Bougainville'.[20] While there is no doubt in Carter's profound knowledge of the former, Pennington's statement about the latter seems far from accurate.

This section looks at the Bluestocking drawing room as a space for learned conversations on travel and exploration and discusses the Bluestockings' connections with the most renowned of eighteenth-century travellers, explorers and geographers. It aims to show various aspects of their interaction and determine the role the Bluestockings played in the diffusion of geographical knowledge. The section sheds more light on the motives behind the Bluestockings' interest in the reading, writing and collecting of travel accounts.

In the poem *Bas Bleu*, which was written in 1783, widely circulated in script and eventually published in 1786, Hannah More praised the cultivated

---

[18] H. More, 'The Bas Bleu: or, Conversation' in H. More, *Florio: A Tale, for Fine Gentlemen and Fine Ladies: and, The Bas Bleu; or, Conversation: Two Poems* (London: Cadell, 1786), p. 82.

[19] M. Pennington, *Memoirs of the Life of Mrs. Elizabeth Carter, with a New Edition of Her Poems*, vol. 1 (London: Rivington, 1816), pp. 16–17.

[20] Pennington, *Memoirs of the Life of Mrs. Elizabeth Carter*, p. 17.

atmosphere of the Bluestocking drawing room in the 1780s and paid homage to the celebrated hostess Elizabeth Vesey. The poem vividly depicts numerous visitors and friends at her widely known conversation parties:

> Here sober Duchesses are seen,
> Chaste Wits, and Critics void of spleen;
> Physicians, fraught with real science,
> And Wigs and Tories in alliance;
> Poets, fulfilling Christian duties,
> Just Lawyers, reasonable Beauties;
> Bishops who preach, and Peers who pay,
> And Countesses who seldom play;
> Learn'd Antiquaries, who, from college,
> Reject the rust, and bring the knowledge;
> And hear it, age, believe it, youth,
> Polemics, really seeking truth;
> And Travellers of that rare tribe,
> Who've *seen* the countries they describe.[21]

At first glance, this group of attendants might seem rather eclectic. However, such diversity is highly suggestive of a wide range of topics that might have been discussed there. Indeed, conversations went far beyond the discussions of the latest novels, poems or memoirs and encompassed the Duchess of Devonshire's election canvassing, volcanoes in Sicily, air balloon ascending and pyramids in Egypt among others. Recent research has shown how the Bluestockings produced and used their knowledge of natural history – botany, conchology, zoology, mineralogy – in their 'intense and intimate engagement with art making and collecting practices',[22] as well as how 'processes of collecting and crafting served to map a complex and rapidly expanding material world within an elite

---

[21] More, 'The Bas Bleu', p. 78.

[22] B.F. Tobin, 'Bluestockings and the Cultures of Natural History' in D. Heller (ed.), *Bluestockings Now!* 56.

domestic environment.'[23] With this in mind, it is possible to assume that the travellers' experiences of distant and near lands and their informative and entertaining oral and printed travel accounts were of considerable interest to the Bluestockings, who readily absorbed and transmitted the knowledge that was circulating in London's intellectual circles. Two laconic lines about 'Travellers of that rare tribe' in More's poem give ground for asking who those travellers were and whether they attended other women-presided intellectual gatherings. The Bluestockings' connections with contemporary geographers, explorers and travellers seem important in many respects if we want to link them with the world of travel and travel writing.

Our analysis of Mary Hamilton's diaries has shown that various subjects pertinent to home and foreign travel were frequently discussed in her circle; numerous brief records of conversations with her well-travelled friends and relations bespeak the young Bluestocking's zest for knowledge about the world. Mary conversed with her uncle Sir William Hamilton on his journey through Wales and Scotland in 1784[24] and on Italy and Russia at various times. The passionate collector, connoisseur of ancient art, volcanologist and His Majesty's envoy to Naples, Sir William invited his niece and her future husband John Dickenson to Italy, urging that they stay for a year or two; he thought that 'nothing opened the *mind* more' than travels, particularly in those people 'who had natural taste & observation'.[25] Mary Hamilton listened to the descriptions of many places in Scotland shared by the poet and politician Richard Glover;[26] she discussed advantages and disadvantages of the Grand Tour with the retired diplomat Robert Gunning.[27] The young woman recorded her conversations with Margaret Cavendish Bentinck, the Duchess of Portland (hereafter interchangeably referred to as Bentinck or the Duchess of Portland) on Spa,[28] her aunt Lady Warwick on Switzerland[29] and Charlotte Walsingham on romantic views in Derbyshire.[30] The diplomat and politician David Murray, Lord Stormont,

---

[23] M. Pelling, 'Collecting the World: Female Friendship and Domestic Craft at Bulstrode Park', *Journal for Eighteenth-Century Studies*, 41.1 (2018), 101.

[24] HAM/2/13, 17 August 1784. [25] HAM/2/14, 30 August 1784.

[26] HAM/2/6, 9 March 1784. [27] HAM/2/2, 4 June 1783. [28] HAM/2/3.

[29] HAM/2/6, 23 December 1783. [30] HAM/2/9, 21 March 1784.

who had resided on the Continent for many years, described 'different *stiles* and *manners* in foreign countries' and shared first-hand impressions of Vienna and Paris where he had lived.[31] It can be argued that numerous oral travel reports from her relations and friends formed a solid base of the young woman's knowledge of the world; they also signal the ongoing oral culture of acquiring information related to travel and geography in the late Georgian period.

It should be pointed out that the 'eighteenth century was one of extraordinary geographical discovery' and exploration was considered a 'primary source of knowledge'.[32] The gathering of scientific information on little-known regions of the world went hand in hand with the taking possession of them and the 'state-sponsored research and discovery expeditions mounted by the British, French, and Russians' established 'the nexus between knowledge and power'.[33] Simultaneously, significant improvements in transport, road systems and infrastructure in Britain and on the Continent considerably facilitated home and foreign journeys for education, health or recreation. The Bluestocking women were not immune to the advancements and trends of the day, and their enthusiasm for travel was constantly growing. In addition, the Bluestockings' frequent interaction with energetic and dedicated travellers and their lively conversation about far and near lands must have acted as the catalyst in activating the educated female audience's interest in travel and travelogues.

Travel writing was a popular genre in the second half of the eighteenth century. Several literary men, who had close links with the Bluestockings, were the authors of at least one travelogue. The names to be mentioned in the first instance are those of the celebrated lexicographer Samuel Johnson (1709–84); his biographer James Boswell (1740–95); the linguist of Italian origin Giuseppe Baretti (1719–89) and music historian Charles Burney (1726–1814), father to the writer Frances Burney and naval officer and

---

[31] HAM/2/12.

[32] D. Outram, *The Enlightenment*, 3rd ed. (New York: Cambridge University Press, 2013), p. 54.

[33] J. Osterhammel, *Unfabling the East: The Enlightenment's Encounter with Asia* (Princeton and Oxford: Princeton University Press, 2018), p. 11.

explorer James Burney. All four men authored travelogues which were published in their lifetime and favourably received by the general reading public.[34] This section takes a different direction and offers to expand the group of travel writers in the Bluestocking salon by focusing on those eminent travellers and explorers of the period whose connections with the Bluestockings have been less studied or have not received scholarly attention to date.

Traveller, historian and writer Nathaniel Wraxall (1751–1831) seems to have been a frequent guest in the Bluestockings' London homes in periods free from travel. His friend, the intellectual William Weller Pepys, befriended Montagu, More and other Bluestockings; Pepys also hosted conversation parties. Wraxall acknowledged that Pepys had introduced him to the Bluestocking circle, an 'assembly of distinguished persons' of the day.[35] Eventually, the traveller's visits to the Bluestockings' drawing rooms resulted in one of the liveliest contemporary descriptions of these accomplished women.[36] Wraxall's long letters to Pepys, in which the travel writer related his extensive continental journeys including the 'Tour round the Baltic',[37] reveal his passion for travel:

> You, a husband, a father, a domestic man, retired, occupy'd
> in Schemes of Education and family concerns; Myself,
> returning from Poland and Hungary and Austria and Italy

---

[34] S. Johnson, *A Journey to the Western Islands of Scotland* (1775); J. Boswell, *An Account of Corsica, the Journal of a Tour to That Island* (1768); J. Boswell, *The Journal of a Tour to the Hebrides, with Samuel Johnson, LL.D.* (1785); G. Baretti, *An Account of the Manners and Customs of Italy* (1768); G. Baretti, *A Journey from London to Genoa, through England* (1770); C. Burney, *The Present State of Music in France and Italy: or, The Journal of a Tour through Those Countries* (1771); C. Burney, *The Present State of Music in Germany, the Netherlands, and United Provinces: or, The Journal of a Tour through Those Countries* (1773).

[35] *A Later Pepys: The Correspondence of Sir William Weller Pepys*, ed. A.C.C. Gaussen, vol. 1 (London and New York: John Lane, 1904), p. 46.

[36] W. Wraxall, *Historical Memoirs of My Own Time*, vol. 1 (London: Cadell and Davies, 1815), pp. 136–58.

[37] Gaussen, *A Later Pepys*, vol. 2, p. 7.

charmed and delighted with what I have seen, but more desirous and impatient than ever to see what remains to me of Europe. I mean Spain and Sicily and Greece, and Constantinople, as well as to visit all Egypt the Archipelago the Lesser Asia, Syria, the Coast of Barbary.[38]

The traveller also mentioned a letter written to Elizabeth Montagu during his travels and her answer to it.[39]

Frances Burney recorded that Wraxall, 'the northern historian', was among the guests at Pepys's assemblies in 1782 and 1783,[40] at a conversation party held at Lady Rothes's, Pepys's sister-in-law.[41] In 1788, Frances Boscawen mentioned dining with him, Pepys, his brother Sir Lucas Pepys and Lady Rothes.[42] Hamilton documented her conversation with Wraxall at one of Vesey's meetings and her impression of the traveller, 'I had an hours [sic] conversation with Mr Wraxall at Mrs Vesey's – he appeared to me a *pretty kind of Man*, one who gives equivocal answers to Ladies till he discovers their sentiments; one who under an affectation of diffidence had a prodigious high opinion of himself.'[43] The diary entry also reveals Hamilton's critical judgement, particularly when the conversation moved on to discuss Spa and other places in the Low Countries which the Bluestocking had visited earlier (Section 4 discusses Hamilton's journal of her travel to Spa):

Lady Dartrey sat next me & we happened to mention Spa, Brussells, & other places we had been at together. M^r

[38] Gaussen, *A Later Pepys*, vol. 2, pp. 45–6.

[39] Gaussen, *A Later Pepys*, vol. 2, pp. 30, 39, 44.

[40] M. D'Arblay, *Diary and Letters of Madame D'Arblay*, vol. 2 (London: Henry Colburn, 1842), pp. 129–30, 294.

[41] D'Arblay, *Diary and Letters of Madame D'Arblay*, vol. 2, p. 209.

[42] C. Aspinall-Oglander, *Admiral's Widow: Being the Life and Letters of the Hon. Mrs. Edward Boscawen From 1761 to 1805* (London: The Hogarth Press, 1942), p. 132.

[43] DDX 274/18.

W. [Wraxall] joined in the conversation & questioned me ab^t the Churches & Pictures in the same manner as any person would do who had never seen them. Pray Miss Hamilton wch are esteem'd the finest? &c &c I replied very civilly, that I was surprised that a Gentleman who was so well informed should enquire. This silenced him. I do not pretend to decry ye merits of Mr W. as an Author – but I think one may discover in his travels through the Northern parts of Europe that he is self sufficient & loose principled.[44]

Another traveller, frequently seen at the Bluestocking gatherings, was the eminent geographer, cartographer and author of scholarly publications on India, James Rennell (1742–1830), also known as Major Rennell. A friend of Joseph Banks and William Pepys, he was a welcome guest and highly knowledgeable partner in conversation. A passage from one of Rennell's letters to Pepys gives an idea of how contemporary travelogues could have been discussed by the geographer at the conversation parties:

> I have begun to read Volney's Travels in Egypt and Syria; and have read two-thirds of the first Vol. and dipt into the 2nd. It is, I think, by far the best book of Travels that has been published for a great many years. Filled with good matter, and pleasantly written. Savary trod (partly) the same path: but he writes like a Frenchman;[45] Volney like an Englishman. If you have leisure to read it, you might be informed and amused. I am seldom amused unless I am informed at the same time.[46]

Charles Burney was well acquainted with Rennell. In a letter to his daughter Frances in 1791, the musicologist informed her, 'Major Rennell has been so kind as to give me a copy of the memoir belonging to his admirable map of

---

[44] DDX 274/18.

[45] J. Rennell discussed *Travels through Syria and Egypt in the Years 1783, 1784, and 1785* by C.-F. Volney and *Letters on Egypt* by C.E. Savary.

[46] Gaussen, *A Later Pepys*, vol. 2, p. 89.

Hindostan,[47] which is out of print. It teaches more about India than all the books besides that have ever been written. I think you will voraciously devour this. It is Dr Robertson's great resource in the disquisitions he has lately published on India.'[48]

The same year, Frances Burney mentioned Rennell's presence at Ann Ord's and Elizabeth Montagu's gatherings. In 1792, the celebrated author of *Camilla* and *Cecilia* went to another conversation party at Ord's which was attended by Rennell and Hamilton (recorded under her married name 'Mrs Dickenson') among others. The guests discussed 'the East India letters from Lord Conwallis, and Major Rennell was there our oracle'.[49] Burney praised his manner of talking and thought that the geographer had 'a plain, unadorned way of giving information' which was 'both pleasant and masterly'.[50] Her usage of the word 'oracle' indicates Rennell's unquestioned expertise and impressive rhetorical skills and the audience's respect for the explorer. One of Hannah More's comments indirectly signals the expertise level of geographical knowledge exchange at the conversation parties and clearly indicates that learned conversations on geographical subjects could be intellectually challenging. In a letter to one of her sisters, the writer used gentle humour to describe her conversation with two travellers at one of Pepys's gatherings. The Bluestocking did not mention the names of her eloquent conversation partners, but it is almost certain that they were Wraxall and Rennell:

> It was my lot the other day at dinner to sit between two travellers, famous for making geography their whole subject; the one is as fond of talking of the east as the other is of the north; the former poured the Ganges into one of my ears, and the latter the Danube into the other, and the confluence of these two mighty rivers deluged all my ideas till I did not know what they were talking about.[51]

---

[47] Burney referred to Rennell's *Memoir of a Map of Hindoostan* (1783).

[48] D'Arblay, *Diary*, vol. 5, p. 261. [49] D'Arblay, *Diary*, vol. 5, p. 300.

[50] D'Arblay, *Diary*, vol. 5, p. 300.

[51] W. Roberts, *Memoirs of the Life and Correspondence of Mrs. Hannah More*, vol. 1 (New York: Harper & Brothers, 1835), p. 238.

The Bluestockings' diaries and memoirs suggest that interaction between travellers and the accomplished women was not necessarily limited to the discussing of or listening to their travel reports. Burney's *Diary and Letters* illustrate to what extent good social skills and 'polite manners' were important for male guests at the meetings presided by the Bluestocking women. For instance, the writer praised Rennell's pleasant manners at one of the crowded public breakfasts which were regularly held at Montagu's house:

> The crowd of company was such that we could only slowly make way in any part. There could not be fewer than four or five hundred people. It was like a full Ranelagh by daylight. . . . We met friends and acquaintance every other step. Amongst them, Major Rennell, whom I always like to meet. . . . I had a very good beau in Major Rennell, who took charge of any catering and regale.[52]

Other travel writers who visited the Bluestocking gatherings were mentioned in their letters and diaries; the 'professional' traveller and author of *Travels through Spain* Henry Swinburne (1743–1803) was among them. Describing a dinner at Garrick's house in London, Hannah More informed her sister:

> We have had a numerous party to dinner; among others, Mr & Mrs Swinburne the travellers, with whom I am lately become much acquainted; they are people who have been a good deal distinguished in different courts. The lady is the more agreeable of the two, though she has not, like her husband, written three quarto volumes about Spain and Calabria. They live chiefly abroad, and are great bigots of popery. She is the great friend of the Queen of Naples and not less a favourite of the Queen of France – a singular pair of friendships for an English woman of no rank.[53]

[52] D'Arblay, *Diary*, vol. 5, pp. 303–5. [53] Roberts, *Memoirs*, vol. 1, pp. 241–2.

Visitors to the Bluestocking assemblies included Jonas Hanway (1712–86) who published the *Historical Account of British Trade over the Caspian Sea, with a Journal of Travels* in 1753. Frances Burney recorded his presence at one of Ord's meetings in 1783, noting that 'Jonas Hanway, the old traveller' was 'very loquacious, extremely fond of talking of what he has seen and heard'.[54]

Interaction with travellers and explorers encompassed a range of inter-linked practices; it included the collective viewing of drawings and examin-ing of specimens and artefacts brought from numerous journeys or voyages. These practices enabled the Bluestockings to become better acquainted with 'new' regions, people and cultures through visualisation and/or physical contact with various material objects. It is particularly true of their encoun-ters with renowned scientific travellers who represented two worlds – those of travel and science – singularly intertwined in the eighteenth century. The long-standing president of the Royal Society Sir Joseph Banks (1743–1820) and members of the 'Banksian Learned Empire'[55] such as the Swedish naturalist and explorer Daniel Solander (1733–82), naturalist John Lightfoot (1735–88), volcanologist Sir William Hamilton (1730–1803) and mineralogist Charles Greville (1749–1809) visited the Bluestocking homes and attended their conversation parties; they were connected with some of the Bluestocking women through either scientific collaboration and shared interests or family ties. Delany's correspondence offers a rare glimpse into these practices and demonstrates how well informed the Bluestockings were in that period. In a letter addressed to her brother Bernard Granville, the celebrated author of the *Flora Delanica* recorded how she and the Duchess of Portland visited Banks's house soon after they had returned from James Cook's *Endeavour* voyage (1768–71):

> We were yesterday together at Mr. Banks's to see some of
> the fruits of his travels, and were delighted with paintings of

---

[54] D'Arblay, *Diary*, vol. 2, p. 231.

[55] D.P. Miller, 'Between Hostile Camps: Sir Humphry Davy's Presidency of the Royal Society of London, 1820–1827', *The British Journal for the History of Science*, 16 (1983), 2.

the Otaheitie plants, quite different from anything the Duchess *ever* saw, so they must be very new to me! They [Banks and Solander] have brought the seeds of some of them which they think will do here; several of them are blossoms of *trees* as big as the largest *oak*, and so covered with flowers that their beauty can hardly been imagined; there is one in particular (the name I cannot recollect), that bears vast flowers, larger and somewhat of the appearance of the largest poppy when full blown, the leaves all fungid; the petals that are like threads, are at the calyx *white*, by degrees shaded with pale *purple*, ending with *crimson*. The leaf of the tree large and of a fine green; the branches are frequently full of a little blue parrot, not bigger than a bullfinch, and they snap off the flowers so fast that the ground is quite strewed with them, they blow daily like the gum cistus. They have a number of very pretty plants that grow out of other trees (like our mistletoe), but with lovely pretty flowers. Most of the views Mr. Banks and Dr. Solander brought over were gone to be engraven for the history of their travels to come out next year; the Natural History will not come out till three years hence, that is, not till they return again. ... I wish my tedious description has not tired you, but I was so pleased with the flower, &c., I could not help communicating it: one extraordinary beauty I forgot, which is that the flower as it hangs down is *transparent*.[56]

A day later in a letter to her niece, Delany focused on describing the Tahitian clothes which she might have thought to have been of more interest to her female relation; the passage was accompanied by her drawing:

> We had last Monday at Mr Banks's house in New Burlington Street, a charming entertainment of oddities, but not half

---

[56] Llanover, *The Autobiography*, vol. 1, pp. 384–5.

time enough. In the first place we saw the Otaheite dress,
something more simple, but not so well suited to our
climate, as our compounded dress. They only wear
a mantle, which they tie about their neck, much of
a square that hangs almost to the ground, so, one arm bare
and the hair tied up in a knot; this is their common dress,
their commanders are distinguished, with a little more orna-
ment, a gorget made of pigeon's feathers and dog-fish teeth.
Feathers in their heads, and caps almost as top gallant as
a modern English lady's.[57]

Other Bluestockings shared Bentinck's and Delany's lively interest in
Tahitian culture; the Tahiti-themed dress which Thrale Piozzi wore at court
convincingly shows how women intellectuals could fully utilize their crea-
tivity, knowledge and connections with explorers for their efficient self-
presentation. In January 1781, the *Morning Herald* informed readers,
'Mrs. Thrale appeared in a striped satin Otaheite pattern, trimmed with
crape, gold lace, and foil, and ornamented with a profusion of stones, of
a new composition, very little interior in point of luster to the most brilliant
jewels, – the *toute ensemble* of this dress was magnificent as well as
singular!'[58] In her diary entitled *Thraliana*, Thrale Piozzi noted with evident
satisfaction:

My Name has figured finely in the Newspapers on Acc^t of
my going to Court on the Birthday in the *O'why'hee* pattern
Silk: the Truth is I had a Mind partly to please the Burneys,
whose Captain [James Burney] brought me some Curiosities
from the South seas, & new discoverd Regions, particularly
a Scrap of Cloth torn from the back of the Indian who killed
Captn Cook with His Club. This Stuff I thought so pretty,
that I got Carr the Mercer to imitate it in Satten; & trimmed

---

[57] Llanover, *The Autobiography*, vol. 1, p. 387.

[58] Cited in J.L. Clifford, *Hester Lynch Piozzi (Mrs. Thrale)*, 2nd ed. (Oxford:
Oxford University Press, 1987), p. 194.

it with Feather'd Ornaments to keep up the Taste of the
Character, still preserving in View the Fashion of the Times.
It was violently admired to be sure, and celebrated in all the
Papers of the Day: – which I have a Notion was owing to
my own willingness to be look'd at.[59]

Thrale Piozzi's 'gesture' deserves our attention as it demonstrates her
many varied motivations behind commissioning and wearing the garment.
The Bluestocking does not seem to have been deeply preoccupied to please
the Burney family; she sought to demonstrate her creative abilities and
originality of thinking, achieve visibility at court and become talked of in
society. Thrale Piozzi's act had a symbolic meaning: she manifested her
loyalty and support of recent Crown acquisitions in the Pacific region. On
the whole, this episode reveals how British women, through their use of
'exotic' elements in clothes, might signal the 'immediate' cultural appro-
priation of newly discovered lands. In such a way, they could add to the
nation's colonial narrative and symbolically contribute to the incorporation
of recently colonised territories into the rising British Empire.

The Bluestockings' letters contain references to newly acquired information in the world of geography. For instance, Delany informed her niece
about Banks and Solander's recent tour to Iceland and the western islands of
Scotland; she had learned many details from John Lightfoot, Bulstrode's
chaplain and curator to the Bentinck's famed collection of natural history:

He [Lightfoot] told me he had seen Mr. Banks and Solander,
and they gave him an account of what was most remarkable
in their summer's tour; amongst other things the discovery
of an island on the western coast of Scotland, called Staffa,
about three miles in circumference, and supported like
a table on a frame by clustered pillars exactly of the form
of those of the Giants' Causeway, and of the same kind of
stone, differing as they do in their angles and dimensions,

---

[59] *Thraliana: The Diary of Mrs. Hester Lynch Thrale (Later Mrs. Piozzi) 1776–1809*,
ed. K.C. Balderston, vol. 1 (Oxford: Clarendon Press, 1942), pp. 480–1.

and some 60 and 70 feet high, their base in the water; and as they sailed round the island they discovered a cave of a very particular form, three hundred yards long, diminishing to the end as an avenue appears to do at a distance; broken pillars on each side from which they might have stept from stone to stone to the end, and the base of pillars made a roof over head. From thence they went to Iceland, which is 65 degrees north latitude, not far from Greenland: there they met with a mountain called Hecla, that had been a volcano, for the country all around it is covered with lava. At the foot of it is a fountain called Geyser, that throws up a stream or column of water 30 feet in diameter, and 64 high. They threw a dead partridge into it, which was very well boyled in seven minutes.[60]

The previously cited passages from Delany's letters reveal the chains through which the news related to travel and discovery flew and allow us to locate the Bluestocking in them, defining her role as that of the 'spreader of innovation'.[61] The passages are also telling of how orality and epistolarity, alongside manuscript exchange and printed publications, served the pathways which ensured rapid dissemination of newly discovered scientific facts, objects and evidence.

Frances Burney, who met Solander at one of Thrale Piozzi's parties in 1780, described him as a 'very sociable' man, 'full of talk, information, and entertainment';[62] the scientist gave 'a very particular account to the company of Captain Cook's appearance at Khamschatka.'[63] In that period, the Bluestockings read and discussed numerous reports on the state-sponsored expedition which were constantly updating via print or word of mouth. The Burneys, whose family member James Burney participated in Cook's voyages, eagerly collected every piece of information they could. In 1780,

---

[60] Llanover, *The Autobiography*, vol. 1, p. 491.

[61] D. Heller, S. Heller, 'A Copernican Shift; or, Remapping the Bluestocking Heavens' in D. Heller, *Bluestockings Now*, 40.

[62] D'Arblay, *Diary*, vol. 1, p. 305. [63] D'Arblay, *Diary*, vol. 1, p. 306.

Burney recorded in her diary, 'Lord Sandwych told my father that the journal of Captain Cook is arrived, and now in the hands of the king, who has desired to have the first perusal of it. I am very impatient to know something of its contents. The ships are both expected almost daily. They have already been out a year longer than was intended.'[64] The Bluestockings kept their finger on the pulse of other ongoing and prospective travels. In her letter to John Dewes in July 1773, Delany communicated that the Duchess of Portland had been to Oxford and met with 'an excellent botanist, Mr Sheffield, keeper of the Museum at Oxford' who was going to Ireland 'to explore all the plants that are *natives* of the place'.[65] In the same letter, she wrote about Banks and Lightfoot's plans to go 'to the top of Snowdon and the Isle of Anglesey' in company with Charles Greville, who was 'far gone in the pursuit of natural curiosities'.[66] Later in October, the Bluestocking mentioned Lightfoot's return from Wales and noted that the 'Welsh expedition has added to his knowledge and our entertainment.'[67]

A series of letters between Delany and Boscawen and between Delany and her brother Granville bear evidence of the Bluestockings' assistance in the organising of scientific travel. In 1774, two women discussed Lightfoot's tour to Cornwall and their help with some practicalities. In July, Boscawen informed Delany that she had sent to Mr. Rashleigh, her steward in Cornwall, 'an explanatory letter concerning Mr. Lightfoot, his purposes and the objects of his journey' and assured that the man could be useful to the naturalist 'in giving him passports to farmers for lodging and good hospitality, for there is nothing of a town that way beyond Penzance'.[68] Further, Boscawen gave her recommendations on places to visit and, through her friend, suggested to Lightfoot that he would 'probably go from Mount Edgcumbe to Boconnoc, from thence to Lostwithiel, and there out of the direct road to the Land's End; but, beside that curious travellers are never out of their way, there is *a mine* near St. Austle better worth seeing

---

[64] D'Arblay, *Diary*, vol. 1, p. 414.

[65] Llanover, *The Autobiography*, vol. 1, p. 518.

[66] Llanover, *The Autobiography*, vol. 1, p. 518.

[67] Llanover, *The Autobiography*, vol. 1, p. 566.

[68] Llanover, *The Autobiography*, vol. 2, p. 16.

than any, by reason of the resemblance it bears to the D. of Bridgewater's underground navigation.'[69] In October, Delany informed Granville that Lightfoot 'returned from Cornwall, from whence he has brought *several* curious *wild plants*; but much disappointed with not having been able to get any of curious minerals; and so was I, for he told me if he succeeded I should come in for a little share'.[70] Delany's letter suggests that their interaction was supposed to be mutually beneficial: in return for assistance, Delany could have added mineral samples to her collection. Another letter reveals her satisfaction from having been involved in the travel organisation, 'I have never told you perhaps how much it pleas'd me to know that Mr. Lightfoot was in any shape benefitted by my letters, *mais cela va sans dire*, for surely I shou'd have wish'd to have had the satisfaction of his Cornish tour more compleat, and his researches more successful than they seem to have been.'[71]

Also, Delany's correspondence is indicative of how travel writers cultivated and valued their acquaintance with the Bluestockings, who, owing to their multiple connections, could be helpful during the preparation or promotion of their publications. In this light, Delany's friendly relationship with the Reverend William Gilpin (1724–1804), the celebrated author who introduced the idea of picturesque into the eighteenth-century cultural debate in Britain,[72] is illustrative. Around 1781, the Bulstrode friends – Delany and Bentinck – learned about Gilpin's ambitious publishing project and became acquainted with his manuscript volume through Boscawen's daughter Frances Leveson.[73] Later, Delany informed Hamilton of certain financial problems that the author had met with, which had considerably

---

[69] Llanover, *The Autobiography*, vol. 2, p. 16. Boscawen referred to *The History of Inland Navigations. Particularly those of the Duke of Bridgwater in Lancashire and Cheshire* (1766).

[70] Llanover, *The Autobiography*, vol. 2, p. 39.

[71] Llanover, *The Autobiography*, vol. 2, p. 44.

[72] J. Buzard, 'The Grand Tour and after (1660–1840)' in P. Hulme and T. Youngs (eds.), *The Cambridge Companion to Travel Writing* (Cambridge: Cambridge University Press, 2002), p. 45.

[73] Llanover, *The Autobiography*, vol. 3, p. 38.

complicated the realisation of his project. The Bluestocking 'confessed' she would have stolen to help him. The use of such expressive hyperbole by the elderly woman, respected universally for her piety, is telling of Delany's exceptional appreciation of the project:

> I have been mortified by a disappointment in an entertain-
> ment I was given encouragement to hope for; no less than
> the publication of Mr. Gilpin's Tours, with the drawings,
> *both* so excellent in their way and lost to the public from the
> check of prudence, which will not allow him to run the
> hazard of so great an expence. ... I wish I *cou'd steal* (for
> I fear I shall never *influence*) out of the mischievous banks at
> the gaming tables four or five hundred pounds, and bestow it
> on a work that wou'd do honour, not only to the very
> worthy and ingenious author, but to the country which he
> lives in.[74]

Instead of 'stealing', as one of Lady Dartrey's letters to Hamilton shows, Delany either initiated or actively participated in the subscription project. Lady Dartrey promised Hamilton to 'send our Subscription to her [Delany] for the Clergyman' and informed of other people who wanted to 'send their Subscriptions to M[rs] Delany'.[75] Gilpin became Delany's correspondent and his letters documented how he presented his drawings to Delany and Bentinck, shared his plans for the future publications and thanked the women for their useful remarks.[76] The writer asked Delany to show his manuscript volumes to 'Lord Bute, if you think them worth his perusal'.[77] Moreover, Gilpin's letters recorded that the learned trio of Bulstrode – Bentinck, Lightfoot and Delany – had had an opportunity to get acquainted with his third manuscript volume of what would become *Remarks on Forest Scenery*; they had done it nearly a decade before the book was published. In 1782, Gilpin appreciated Delany's 'desire to see it' and promised that the

---

[74] Llanover, *The Autobiography*, vol. 3, pp. 32–3. [75] HAM/1/11/8.

[76] Llanover, *The Autobiography*, vol. 3, pp. 37–8, 79.

[77] Llanover, *The Autobiography*, vol. 3, p. 79.

volume would 'take the first opportunity to pay its respects' to her. The writer assured that he would send 'the third and last part of my Observations on Forest Scenery' as soon as he received the volume from 'Mr. Blamire's hands, to whom I sent it to be sewed up together' and warned that 'it is not fit to pay visits anywhere else' as the manuscript was still full of 'crudities and imperfections uncorrected'.[78] Later, Delany's unsolicited sharing of the volume with other people caused severe rebukes from the author.[79] Notwithstanding the incident, their communication continued and Gilpin's letters suggest that the writer sent other accounts of his to Delany and, through her, to Bentinck, for which the Duchess of Portland thanked him.[80] In his *Account*, Gilpin acknowledged that Bentinck had 'sent him a note of one hundred pounds as her subscription'. Nevertheless, 'he chose rather . . . to relay on the public . . . and returned the Duchess's note with many thanks for her generosity.' Importantly, Gilpin had intended to dedicate his *Observations on the Lakes* to Bentinck; after her death in 1785, 'he inscribed it to the queen . . . for the kindness which the king and she had shewn to his friend Mrs Delany.'[81]

Gilpin's communication with Delany continued after Bentinck's death, as his letters show. In 1786, Gilpin thanked the Bluestocking for her efforts in promoting his to-be book at the 'highest' level, 'You have *highly gratifyed* me, by telling me ye Queen has approved my book. I can now with some confidence present it to her.'[82] Most likely, Mary Delany, who had friendly relationships with the royal family in the 1780s, had shown Queen Charlotte the manuscript volume of his *Observations on the Lakes* which would appear in print the following year. In his subsequent letters, Gilpin lamented delays in publishing it, 'I yet see no prospect of my book, about which, madam,

---

[78] Llanover, *The Autobiography*, vol. 3, p. 82.

[79] Llanover, *The Autobiography*, vol. 3, pp. 83–4.

[80] Llanover, *The Autobiography*, vol. 3, p. 92.

[81] W. Gilpin, 'An account of the Revd Mr Gilpin, Vicar of Boldre in New Forest, written by himself' in W. Jackson (ed.), *Memoirs of Dr. Richard Gilpin, of Scaleby Castle in Cumberland* (London and Carlisle: B. Quaritch, C. Thurnam, 1879), pp. 142–3.

[82] Llanover, *The Autobiography*, vol. 3, p. 306.

you are so kindly interested.'[83] In May 1786, the writer thanked Delany for the opportunity to see her 'delightful volumes of plants'[84] during his short visit to her,

> Indeed, dear madam, you made us both [Gilpin and his wife] *very happy*. You not only gave us *present* pleasure, but you furnished us with an agreeable topic of conversation during the afternoon, and *strewed flowers* in our way over the barren scenes of Bagshot Heath. . . . I am *now fully* convinced that black is the best ground you could have chosen'.[85]

Mary Delany's correspondence reveals that it was not only William Gilpin who seemed anxious about the excessive pre-publication circulation of his accounts; another eminent traveller was cautious about providing the audience with either written or oral reports of his exploits in Asia and Africa. The case of James Bruce (1730–94), author of *Travels to Discover the Source of the Nile* (1790), deserves our attention in a number of ways. Although evidence of his attendance at the Bluestocking meetings has not been traced, three letters to Samuel Crisp, written by Frances Burney, documented her communication with 'his Abyssinian Majesty' during the explorer's visits to St. Martin's Street in 1775. Burney's father got acquainted with the traveller through a Mrs Strange, as the music historian sought for the information on the 'Theban harp', an ancient Egyptian musical instrument. Bruce shared with the musicologist his drawings and descriptions of the harp and 'an Abyssinian lyre in present use'.[86] Frances recorded that the explorer aroused 'equal curiosity in the most refined and the most uncultivated of his contemporaries' and his 'narration, and even the sight of Mr. Bruce, were . . . vehemently sought, not only by all London,

---

[83] Llanover, *The Autobiography*, vol. 3, p. 340.

[84] Llanover, *The Autobiography*, vol. 3, p. 346.

[85] Llanover, *The Autobiography*, vol. 3, pp. 349–50.

[86] M. d'Arblay, *Memoirs of Doctor Burney, Arranged From His Own manuscripts, From Family Papers, and From Personal Recollections*, vol. 1 (London: Edward Moxon, 1832), p. 297.

but, as far as written intercourse could be stretched, by all Europe'.[87] The 'great man-mountain',[88] as Burney called the Scottish explorer for his height, left a lasting impression on the writer; she not only depicted his portrait but also documented how careful Bruce was about relating his travels to the audience and how defensive he was against the public's excessive attention to him. In the circle of his friends, Burney admitted, 'he is not only chatty and easy, but full of comic and dry humour; though, if any company enters, he sternly ... shuts up his mouth, and utters not a word' because 'he is persuaded that nobody comes near him but either to stare at him as a curiosity, or pick his brains for their own purposes.' Burney acknowledged that 'every word that has been drawn from him has been printed in some newspaper or magazine; which as he intends to publish his travels himself, is abominably provoking; and seems to have made him suspicious of some dark design, or some invidious trick.'[89] Further history of Bruce's travelogue and the contradictory reception of his book, which Section 3 discusses in more detail, prove that there were good reasons behind the explorer's apprehensions. Thrale Piozzi's diary contains an illustrative example that shows how contradictory the judgement of the explorer's stories was. She recorded one of Montagu's parties, held in Brighton in 1780, where 'Bruce of Abyssinia has been greatly ridiculed, particularly for trying to make the World believe that the People in Abyssinia eat cuts from the live Beast; yet Mr Coxe & I found the same thing in an old Book of Travels here at Brighthelmston the other day.'[90] What is important to highlight here is that after Bruce's *Travels* were finally published in 1790, the explorer sought for Frances Burney's assistance to promote his travelogue at court, but she rejected his approaches:

> This extraordinary wight acquainted my father, not long
> since, that he should take the liberty to order a set of his
> Travels to be finely bound up, and sent to 'his daughter with

[87] M. d'Arblay, *Memoirs of Doctor Burney*, vol. 1, p. 296.

[88] M. d'Arblay, *Memoirs of Doctor Burney*, vol. 1, p. 298.

[89] M. d'Arblay, *Memoirs of Doctor Burney*, vol. 1, pp. 300–301.

[90] Balderston, *Thraliana*, vol. 1, p. 453.

the Queen'; because there had appeared, some years ago, an
ode, addressed to himself, which he attributed to that person, and felt eager to acknowledge! Much surprised, my
father inquired further, and heard there was a great compli-
ment to himself, also, which induced this suggestion. My
father said that alone was sufficient to satisfy him it was not
his daughter's.[91]

Thus, unlike eighteenth-century single-gender sites such as coffee
houses, clubs, learned societies and universities, the Bluestocking salon –
a gender-mixed intellectual space presided by the accomplished women
with numerous connections – provided travel writers and explorers with
access to an educated female audience. As oral performance has always been
in the centre of the 'making of knowledge'[92] and the period was marked by
the possibility to achieve a high status 'not through publishing, but through
personal contacts and correspondence',[93] the participation in the
Bluestocking gatherings should be considered an activity which British
travellers and explorers found useful in at least two ways. It was beneficial
to their scholarly status and publishing career as the Bluestocking drawing
rooms furnished travellers with the intellectual setting where they could
share geographical knowledge with a wider circle of people, discuss their
travel reports and experiences, introduce newly discovered facts and data
and exchange ideas about the latest travelogues. Also, the attendance at the
Bluestocking gatherings could add to travellers' profiles, allowing them to
expand their social network and maintain old connections. Travellers'
attendance at these parties indicates the awareness of the 'learned' status
of the Bluestockings, their visibility in contemporary society and their
instrumentality in knowledge dissemination. The Bluestocking diaries and
correspondence demonstrate that these accomplished women could approve
and support travellers' scientific and writing projects, promote published

---

[91] D'Arblay, *Diary*, vol. 5, p. 109.

[92] J.A. Secord, 'How Scientific Conversation Became Shop Talk', *Transactions of
the Royal Historical Society*, Sixth Series, 17 (2007), 130.

[93] Secord, 'How Scientific Conversation Became Shop Talk', 134.

travel accounts and facilitate their reception by the wider public. On the other hand, through interaction with British travellers and explorers, the Bluestockings stayed in the centre of the making of contemporary geographical knowledge. Numerous conversations on geographical subjects, which were held in London's drawing rooms, contributed to the Bluestockings' knowledge of the world and stimulated their 'appetite' for the reading, writing and collecting of travel accounts.

3 Reading Travelogues

> Some time after, turning suddenly to me, he [Samuel Johnson]
>   said,
> 'Miss Burney, what sort of reading do you delight in?
> History? – travels? – poetry? – or romances?'[94]

In August 1778, Samuel Johnson asked Frances Burney about her reading interests and whether she read travelogues; the timorous writer, as her
Diary and Letters suggest, evaded the question, fearing to be further
examined by the celebrated lexicographer. Section 3 attempts to find
answers to these and other questions related to the reading of travel
accounts in the Bluestocking circle. Did they frequently read about travels?
What were their expectations of the genre? Which travelogues did these
sophisticated female readers prioritise? What were their reading practices?
This section analyses numerous laconic records and passing mentions of
travelogues, scattered across the Bluestockings' diaries and correspondence,
and seeks to depict a collective portrait of the Bluestocking readers of
travels. It offers evidence on their engagement with geographical knowledge and sheds more light on the role which travelogues played in the
intellectual and cultural environment of the period.

Starting from the seventeenth century, travel writing had been a 'key
contributor to the advancement of science'.[95] Explorers who made geographical, botanical and ethnographical discoveries and informed the reading
audience about their scientific expeditions authored many travelogues in the
eighteenth century. The genre was particularly elastic, as boundaries
between academic disciplines remained blurred and indistinct. Travel narrative of the period amalgamated lengthy descriptive passages or chapters
pertaining to history, ethnography, natural history, archaeology with
a travel report in the proper sense of the word. Recent research on the
Bluestockings' reading of books in the 1750s has revealed a spectrum of
their interests which, apart from fiction, poetry, drama, history, philosophy,

[94] D'Arblay, *Diary*, vol. 1, p. 92. [95] Thompson, *Travel Writing*, p. 86.

politics, divinity and science, covered geography and travel.[96] The primary record of the Bluestockings' reading, Schellenberg argues, is their voluminous correspondences which document their reading and responses during long absences from the metropolis.[97] This section attempts to show that in the period between 1760 and 1799, the members of the Bluestocking circle read a profusion of travelogues and their reading was systematic, selective and accentuated. Recent publications on travels were always on their radar; news on them spread either by word of mouth or via correspondence. During the decade between 1780 and 1790, the Bluestockings left multiple records of reading travels, which allow us to identify a group of core travelogues that were widely read, recommended and discussed by the Bluestockings in face-to-face and epistolary communication.

One of the core travelogues was William Coxe's *Travels into Poland, Russia, Sweden, and Denmark* (1784). In May 1784, Hamilton recorded that Walpole had conversed about the book at one of Vesey's conversation parties; the author's previous publication, *Accounts of Russian Discoveries* (1780), had also been discussed and 'much commended'.[98] Coxe's *Accounts* informed Britons of recent geographical discoveries made by Russians in Siberia, Kamchatka and the northern part of the Pacific Ocean and focused on a secret expedition of Pyotr Krenitsyn and Mikhail Levashev to the eastern Aleutian Islands. Two days later, Hamilton noted that *Travels* were again talked about at Mary Delany's, 'The D^{ss} D^r of Portland Lady Bute Mr Walpole Mr Frederick Montagu came in soon after me the Conversation was sensible & agreeable – they talk'd of Lord Melcombes Diary … mention'd of Coxe Travels.'[99] Walpole's letter addressed to Henry Seymour Conway confirms his fascination with the travelogue, 'Mr. Coxe's Travels are very different: plain, clear, sensible, instructive, and entertaining. It is a noble work, and precious to me who delights in quartos: the two volumes contain twelve hundred pages – I have already devoured a quarter, though I have had them but three days.'[100]

---

[96] Ellis, 'Reading practices', 217–18.   [97] Schellenberg, 'Reading', 26–7.

[98] HAM/2/10, 29 May 1784.   [99] HAM/2/10, 31 May 1784.

[100] H. Walpole, *The Yale Edition of Horace Walpole's Correspondence*, eds. W.S. Lewis et al., vol. 39 (New Haven and London: Yale University Press, 1937–83), p. 413.

Reading these lines, it is easy to imagine how the author of *The Castle of Otranto* might have expressed his opinion about the travelogue in Vesey's or Delany's drawing rooms.

Mary Hamilton's diary and epistolary records allow us to reconstruct her reading of Coxe's *Travels* in the autumn of 1784 when she was on a three-month visit to the Duchess of Portland at Bulstrode, '[27 October] read in Coxe . . . [later] read as usual in Cox'; '[6 November] I read for 2 hours to the D[uche]^{ss} & M^{rs} D[elany] in Coxes Travels'; '[11 November] Finish'd the 2^{d} Vol: Quarto of Coxes Travels this Eve[nin]g'.[101] In a long journal letter, written from Bulstrode and addressed to the courtier Charlotte Gunning, the Bluestocking asked her friend if she had read the book and wanted to learn her opinion on it, 'I want to know if you have read Coxes Tour through Poland Russia &c, and how you like it, I am reading it to the Dear friends [Delany and Bentinck] in an Eve[nin]g, and have almost get through the first Volume, I like it very well on the whole & He appears an impartial writer.' In the same journal letter two weeks later, Hamilton informed Gunning of her progress in reading the book, 'I am going on prosperously wth Coxe being in 355 page of the 2d Vol. – sometimes he amuses me, *sometimes* informs me, and sometimes makes me Yawn, he is I believe to be depended upon, as there appears an air of veracity in every thing he relates.'[102] The letter reveals how well informed Mary Hamilton was; in it, the young woman shared some details of Coxe's current travel project, 'he is now gone with Mr Whitebread (the great Brewers Son) – they are to travel through the Northern Courts and Mr W[hitebread] allows Mr Coxe £800 per An[num]: besides paying all travelling and other expenses.'[103]

In her letter to Montagu in July 1784, Carter acknowledged that she had been thinking of reading Coxe's *Travels* and complained that it would be 'a formidable undertaking'.[104] Yet, in September, after having received

---

[101] HAM/2/14. [102] HAM/1/15/2/31.

[103] HAM/1/15/2/31. William Coxe accompanied Samuel Whitbread (1764–1815) on his European tour.

[104] *Letters from Mrs. Elizabeth Carter, to Mrs. Montagu, between the Years 1755 and 1800*, vol. 3 (London: F.C. and J. Rivington, 1817), p. 217.

Montagu's positive response on the travelogue, she sounded much more determined to do it, 'From your account of Mr Coxe, I shall certainly borrow him if I live to come to London.'[105] In July, Thrale Piozzi recommended Coxe's *Travels* to her daughter Queeney, 'you will work at it night and day – the Subject – and I think the Style – is much to your natural Taste.'[106] In a letter to More, Pepys also mentioned that he 'had read most of Coxe's Russia'.[107] In 1786, Burney documented her somewhat 'belated' reading of *Travels* which she found informative and useful, 'The style is far from either elegant or pleasing, but they are full of information and historic anecdotes, and seem written with the strictest intention of veracity: – intention, I say, for a foreign traveller can rarely be certain of the truth and justice even of his own observations, much less of those he gathers as he runs.'[108] This diary record reveals her thoughts on such important issues in travel writing as subjectivity and accuracy in authorial interpretation of a foreign environment.

Burney's *Diary and Letters* show that some of the Bluestockings were acquainted with William Coxe. The author of *Evelina* recorded that at a crowded assembly at Mrs Paradise's in 1782, she saw no familiar faces except 'Dr. Solander, Mr. Coxe the traveller'.[109] The same year, the travel writer was among the guests at one of Thrale Piozzi's assemblies.[110] Why was Coxe's travelogue on Russia so widely read by the Bluestockings? Certainly, the author's connections in London's cross-cutting intellectual circles and his acquaintance with the accomplished women added to the popularity of his book with the Bluestockings. On the other hand, there seems to have been other reasons behind it. In the eighteenth century, both countries – Britain and Russia – were empires on the rise that had already colonised vast territories and had an 'appetite' for acquiring more.

[105] *Letters from Mrs. Elizabeth Carter*, vol. 3 p. 223.

[106] *The Piozzi Letters: Correspondence of Hester Lynch Piozzi, 1784–1821 (formerly Mrs. Thrale)*, ed. E.A. Bloom, L.D. Bloom, vol. 1 (Newark: University of Delaware Press; London and Toronto: Associated University Presses, 1989–2002), p. 77.

[107] Gaussen, *A Later Pepys*, vol. 2, p. 232.   [108] D'Arblay, *Diary*, vol. 3, p. 134.

[109] D'Arblay, *Diary*, vol. 2, p. 116.   [110] D'Arblay, *Diary*, vol. 2, p. 162.

However, Russia's territorial acquisitions in the second half of the eighteenth century were more 'impressive' than those of Britain due to the loss of the British North American colonies. Russia's latest expansion – the annexation of Crimea in 1783, inclusion of large territories (parts of present-day Ukraine and Belarus) due to the first partition of Poland in 1772 and ongoing incorporation of the empire's possessions in Asia – attracted the attention of the Bluestockings who read newspapers; discussed politics; and communicated with British politicians, diplomats and foreign envoys at their conversation parties. Besides, three women in the Bluestocking network had close family links with the country's ambassadors to Russia.[111] In her diaries, Hamilton mentioned conversing on Russia with Delany, Bentinck, Gunning and Walsingham as well as Sir William Hamilton, Lord Stormont and Lord Mansfield.

Bluestockings' commentary on Coxe's *Travels* gives an idea of the intellectual female reader's expectations of solid travelogues; they coincided with the period's generic conventions that prescribed travel texts to be informative and entertaining. If simplicity and impartiality added to the positive reception of travel accounts by the Bluestocking audience, their veracity and accuracy were of paramount importance as compilations and fake travel reports were not uncommon in the period. In this sense, the case of James Bruce's travelogue, which was widely read and discussed by the Bluestockings between 1780 and 1790, is an illustrative example; the book divided the readership into two opposite groups. Bruce's travel book (Section 2 discusses Frances Burney's acquaintance with the explorer) provoked much doubt in the audience for its sensational material. Long before it was published, information on the traveller's exploits had leaked out and significantly 'warmed up' public interest in the future publication. In 1787, Walpole wrote to More, 'Bruce is printing his Travels, which I suppose will prove that his narratives were fabulous, as he will scarce

---

[111] Hamilton's aunt Lady Jane Cathcart accompanied her husband Lord Charles Cathcart, the British envoy to Russia (in service 1768–72), to St. Petersburg. Gunning's father Sir Charles Gunning succeeded Cathcart in the post (1772–6). Charlotte Walsingham's father Sir Charles Hanbury Williams, was the British envoy to Russia from 1752 to 1759.

repeat them by the press.'[112] Three years later, the owner of Strawberry Hill House did not change his opinion and expressed it to his friend Conway, 'I stick fast at the beginning of the first volume of Bruce, though I am told it is the most entertaining – but I am sick of his vanity, and (I believe) of his want of veracity, – I am sure of his want of method, and of his obscurity.'[113] Another of Walpole's letters to the same addressee is illustrative of how contradictory the response to the travelogue could have been, 'I do not love disputes, and shall not agree with you about Bruce; but if you like him, you shall not choose an author for me. It is the most absurd, obscure, and tiresome book I know.'[114]

Hannah More read Bruce's travelogue in the year it was published. One of her letters exhibits More's shrewdness and trust in the explorer, 'Plenty of reading here, but not quite time for it. Five volumes of Bruce's Abyssinia [are] on the table. You know he was suspected, but I believe falsely, to have told a thousand extravagancies in these travels.'[115] In 1790, Burney started to read Bruce's travelogue, but it is not clear whether she read the book to the end. The writer noted, 'Dr. Fisher lent me the first volume of Mr. Bruce. But I could only find time to look over the Introduction; which, indeed, in pompous promise of what is to come, and satisfied boast of what has been performed, exceeds whatever yet the most doughty hero has advanced of his own *faicts et* gestes.'[116] Thrale Piozzi also made a record about Bruce and his publication, 'I have not seen Bruce of Abyssinia's Book tho' it is come out, but fear it will end insipidly: like Punch that was too hot at first, they have lower'd the Spirit all away now. He is an odd Man, little respected for Veracity even in his own Country.'[117] The veracity of Bruce's description of Ethiopian political and social life was 'fundamentally accurate',[118] and later expeditions confirmed his observations. The aforementioned diary and epistolary records

[112] Lewis, *Correspondence*, vol. 31, p. 255.

[113] Lewis, *Correspondence*, vol. 39, p. 274.

[114] Lewis, *Correspondence*, vol. 39, p. 275. [115] Roberts, *Memoirs*, vol. 1, p. 349.

[116] D'Arblay, *Diary*, vol. 5, p. 109. [117] Balderston, *Thraliana*, vol. 2, p. 765.

[118] R. Bridges, "Bruce, James (1730–1794): British Traveller' in J. Speake (ed.), *Literature of Travel and Exploration: An Encyclopedia* (London and New York: Routledge, 2013), p. 131.

demonstrate a range of the intellectual reader's response to the sensational travel account of the period – from interest and praise to distrust and rejection.

Although nobody doubted the results of James Cook's first circumnavigation, the Bluestockings' response to *An Account of the Voyages* (1773) was rather reserved. The travelogue was penned by the literary man John Hawkesworth who had been employed by the Admiralty to collate the original travel journals written by Cook, Banks and other explorers and compile an account based on their records. The travelogue was discussed in the Bluestocking epistolary community; Chapone's and Carter's letters reveal their ideas on it. Chapone did not like Hawkesworth's lengthy commentary on navigation subjects and found the book less entertaining than she had expected:

> I have read through Hawksworth's Account of the Voyages of Cooke, &c. I mean as much of them as is readable, for the greater part is only so to navigators. 'Tis a melancholy kind of reading! What an idea does it give one of the state of near half the Globe! ... There is a very small part of this large and expensive work that affords the least entertainment, and some of the reflections and remarks of the author appear to me of very little value. Upon the whole I was, like every body else that I know, who has read the work, rather disappointed. Have you seen it?[119]

It seems that Carter, who had been acquainted with the author for many years and praised his literary abilities,[120] did not venture to read the travelogue because of 'indecent' descriptions in the book. The compilation, which contained information on Tahitian sexual culture,[121] repelled the Bluestocking from reading it:

---

[119] *The Posthumous Works of Mrs. Chapone*, vol. 1 (London: John Murray and A. Constable, 1807), pp. 167–9.

[120] *Letters from Mrs. Elizabeth Carter*, vol. 2, p. 207.

[121] A.M. Thell, *Minds in Motion: Imagining Empiricism in Eighteenth-Century British Travel Literature* (Lewisburg: Bucknell University Press, 2017), pp. 153–6.

You [Montagu] ask me if I have read Banks' and Solander's voyages?[122] I have not, and I believe I never shall. Mrs Howe was so good as to propose sending me the book to Deal, but I have declined it. The account, which you gave me, of the very strong tendency of the preface, (and the same account I have since received from others) and the scandalous indecency of some parts of the book, have raised my indignation, and entirely prevented my feeling any curiosity about it .... My own opinion of the book is not derived from the criticisms in the newspapers, which I scarcely ever read, but from other accounts .... I am told there are many literary inaccuracies; but these are trifles compared with moral offences.[123]

This passage suggests that Carter's decision whether or not to read a travelogue largely depended on the information which circulated within the circle; her friends' recommendations were important for the Bluestocking.

By the time Cook's *Voyages* were published in 1784, the nation had grown fascinated by his epic expeditions, felt proud of the 'progress' of civilisation in distant realms of the world and still grieved his death. Burney's diary reveals her thoughts about the celebrated explorer – his personality, exploits and death – and shows to what extent his image was idealized in that period:

How hard, after so many dangers, so much toil, – to die in so shocking a manner – in an island he had himself discovered – among savages he had himself, in his first visit to them, civilised and rendered kind and hospitable, and in pursuit of obtaining justice in a cause in which he had himself no interest, but zeal for his other captain! He was, besides, the

---

[122] Banks and Solander were on board the *Endeavour* during Cook's first voyage from 1768 to 1771.

[123] *Letters from Mrs. Elizabeth Carter*, vol. 2, p. 209.

most moderate, humane, and gentle circumnavigator who ever went out upon discoveries; agreed the best with all the Indians, and, till this fatal time, never failed, however hostile they met, to leave them his friends ... he boldly went among them without precautions for safety, and paid for his incautious intrepidity with his very valuable life.[124]

In 1780, Anna Seward published her *Elegy on Captain Cook*, which praised his service to both the nation and 'civilised' world:

What Pow'r inspir'd his dauntless breast to brave
The scorch'd Equator, and th' Antartic wave?
Climes, where fierce suns in cloudless ardors shine,
And pour the dazzling deluge round the Line;
The realms of frost, where icy mountains rise,
'Mid the pale summer of the polar skies? –
IT WAS HUMANITY![125]

Writing to Vesey from Deal in 1784, Carter informed the Bluestocking hostess of reading Cook's *Voyages*. She vividly described the pictures her imagination had produced while she had been reading the book:

Have you read Captain Cook's last voyages? I have just finished them. The description of the savage inhabitants of the southern climates is a fine eloge of *a state of nature*, of which one species of philosophers is fond of speaking in such rapturous terms! I was heartily glad to take my leave of these barbarians, and to find myself among the harmless gentle contented race, that dwell on the borders of the arctic circle. Placed on the shore of a frozen ocean, surrounded by mountains of perennial snow, listening to the howl of stormy winds, the bellowing of sea horses, and the growl

---

[124] D'Arblay, *Diary*, vol. 1, p. 304.

[125] Miss Seward, *Elegy on Captain Cook* (London: J. Dodsley, 1780), p. 3.

of hungry bears, these poor people think no country under
heaven so highly favoured as their own.[126]

For Burney and her reading companions at Norbury Park, the reading of
Cook's *Voyages* was a formidable task; she acknowledged that they made
slow progress in reading it out.[127] Hamilton's two diaries contain several
records which documented the process of reading. For the first time, she
mentioned the book on 11 July 1784, noting that Walsingham entertained
her company (Hamilton was one of them) by reading several descriptions
from the travelogue, while the guests were looking over the prints.[128]
Twelve days later, Hamilton recorded, 'Lord Stormont was so good to
lend me the fine Edition of Cooks Voyages 3 Vol. Quarto & also the Set of
Prints belonging to them till they go to Wandsworth Hill.'[129] The young
woman began to read the book only ten days later, and she did it regularly,
'begun Cooks Voyages';[130] 'read in Cooks Voyages'.[131] When Hamilton
suffered from eye inflammation and was not able to continue, her friend
Anna Maria Clarke read it out to her, 'AM read to me in Cookes
Voyages';[132] 'AM read to me till ½ past 10 in Cooks Voyages';[133] 'AM
read to me in Cooks Voyages.'[134] In autumn, Hamilton might not have read
much in the book, as she had gone for a long stay to Bulstrode; she renewed
the efforts on her return to London in December. Hamilton reproached her
fiancé for having distracted her from reading, 'till dinner time [I] read hard
in Cooks Voyages – I have not got through the 1st Vol. & there are 3
Quartos I have been sadly idle as to reading since I quitted Bulstrode – 'tis
Your fault – for I ought to have got through them before I went there, I am
now in a fright for fear Lord Stormont should want them'.[135]

[126] *A Series of Letters between Mrs. Elizabeth Carter and Miss Catherine Talbot, from
the Year 1741 to 1770* (London: F.C. and J. Rivington, 1809), vol. 4, pp. 345–6.

[127] D'Arblay, *Diary*, vol. 2, p. 323. [128] HAM/2/12 11 July 1784.

[129] HAM/2/12 23 July 1784. [130] HAM/2/12 2 August 1784.

[131] HAM/2/14 18 August 1784. [132] HAM/2/14 26 August 1784.

[133] HAM/2/14 27 August 1784. [134] HAM/2/14 29 August 1784.

[135] HAM/2/15 18 January 1785.

Thrale Piozzi's *Observations and Reflections Made in the Course of a Journey Through France, Italy and Germany* (1789) was the only female-authored travel account among the travelogues most popular with the Bluestockings in the 1780s; Section 4 will discuss both the writing and reception of it in detail. Thus, the analysis has shown that all four travelogues were read and discussed within the year of publication; this fact signals the selectivity of the Bluestockings' reading and their efficient navigation in the book market. The timely reading helped them to acquire current geographical knowledge and stay informed about the latest geographical discoveries, expeditions and news in the world of travel. It should be noted that three out of four travelogues – those by Coxe, Bruce and Cook – became Britain's best-selling travel accounts and classics of the genre in the period.

More information on the travelogues read by the Bluestockings between 1760 and 1799 is given in Appendix 1; it contains two lists. The first includes all the travel accounts which were identified as definitely read by the Bluestockings. It also contains the travelogues which Thrale Piozzi mentioned in her *Observations* as well as James Smith's *Sketch of Tour* with her MS notes. The second list represents the travel accounts which were possibly read by the Bluestockings; references to them appear in their letters, diaries and marginalia. On the whole, Appendix 1 lists forty-three titles, thirty-six of which were definitely read by the Bluestockings. The data signal the broad geographical scope that these travel accounts covered and further enforce the argument about the Bluestockings' preference for recent publications. Also, this appendix provides a glimpse into a group of female-authored travelogues, which is composed of six titles. The travel accounts penned by Thrale Piozzi, Montagu, Miller, Vigor, Craven and Du Bocage were identified as those which were definitely read by the Bluestockings. The relatively small number of women's travelogues in the list is explained by the period's scarcity of them. Before 1770, only two female-authored travel accounts – those by Elizabeth Justice on Russia and Mary Wortley Montagu on Turkey – appeared in print, and around twenty women's travelogues were published in the last thirty years of the eighteenth century.[136] On the other hand, the Bluestockings do not seem

---

[136] K. Turner, *British Travel Writers in Europe 1750–1800: Authorship, Gender and National Identity* (Aldershot and Burlington: Ashgate, 2001), p. 127.

to have given special preference for women's travel books as no specific reference to either has been traced so far. Vigor's and Craven's travelogues were the descriptions of their residence and travel in the Russian Empire, respectively. The fact of reading both books may serve as additional proof of the Bluestockings' special interest in travel accounts on Russia. It also gives ground to suggest that their choice of books might have depended rather on a certain country or region which travelogues related than on the author's gender. Moreover, the Bluestockings' critical judgement of these female-authored travelogues was not always positive. If Talbot considered Montagu's *Letters* on Turkey 'very amusing ... and I dare say genuine'[137] and Delany thought of Vigor's *Letters* as 'natural and informing',[138] Thrale Piozzi found Craven's *Journey* more entertaining than informative, 'Lady Craven's Tour too is exquisitely pretty, and will be read with Delight while Tournefort lies by for another Age in which Information may once more grow welcome.'[139] She was also critical of Du Bocage's *Letters on England* and thought that 'her Information has been miserably confined ... & many of her Facts are false.'[140] Interestingly, Thrale Piozzi read this travelogue in Paris, so it was most likely its French edition. It should be noted that although the Bluestocking did not refer to Miller's *Letters* in her *Observations*, she had been acquainted with the author; together with Burney, Thrale Piozzi had attended her literary gatherings in Bath in 1780.[141] References to reading Helen Maria Williams's *Letters Written in France* (1790) and *Letters Containing a Sketch of the Politics of France* (1795) as well as Sarah Murray's *Companion, and Useful Guide to the Beauties of Scotland* (1799) have not been traced and, therefore, included into Appendix 1, though these female-authored publications should be mentioned here as Thrale Piozzi owned them in her home library (see Appendixes

---

[137] *A Series of Letters*, vol. 3, p. 33.

[138] Llanover, *The Autobiography*, vol. 2, p. 217.

[139] Balderston, *Thraliana*, vol. 2, p. 730. Thrale Piozzi referred to Joseph Pitton de Tournefort's *Relation d'un voyage du Levant* (1717), which was translated into several languages and widely read in Europe.

[140] *The French Journals of Mrs. Thrale and Dr.* Johnson, ed. M. Tyson and H. Guppy (Manchester: The Manchester University Press, 1932), p. 91.

[141] D'Arblay, *Diary*, vol. 1, pp. 363–5.

4 and 5). Taking into consideration her communication with Williams as well as her interest in Scotland and intention to publish her Scottish journal, it is more than probable that the Bluestocking also read these books.

Several references which were cited in Sections 2 and 3 reveal that information on recent publications was frequently received by the Bluestockings from either travel writers and explorers or other members of their circle by word of mouth; recommendations were given via epistolary communication as well. In 1763, Talbot informed Carter that Elizabeth Montagu had been the first to tell her about Mary Wortley Montagu's *Letters*.[142] Boscawen, who frequently shared her opinion of books with Delany, recommended the recently published travelogue by Boswell, which she found suitable for recreational reading out in the evening, 'We are much entertained with Mr. Boswell's tour to the Hebrides; if your knotting is ever at leisure to be read to, I think you will be amus'd with this book, which will not require so much attention as lectures on higher subjects, and thus may be proper for an evening hour.'[143] The literary men, closely associated with the Bluestocking circle, were also highly enthusiastic about recommending travelogues. In this respect, Charles Burney's letter to his daughter Frances that mentioned four books of the genre is illustrative:

> I have idly got into miscellaneous reading – the Correspondence of Voltaire, Soame Jenyn's works, Aikin's Poems, Mr. Beckford's 'Jamaica', two volumes. ... Major Rennell has been so kind as to give me a copy of the memoir belonging to his admirable map of Hindostan, which is out of print. It teaches more about India than all the books besides that have ever been written. I think you will voraciously devour this. It is Dr. Robertson's great resource in the disquisitions he has lately published on India. I have likewise just got Rochon's 'Voyage a Madagascar, et aux Indes Orientales,' which I like very much.[144]

[142] *A Series of Letters*, vol. 3, p. 33.

[143] Llanover, *The Autobiography*, vol. 3, p. 296.

[144] D'Arblay, *Diary*, vol. 5, pp. 260–1.

Also, some Bluestockings who had close links with London's publishers could obtain first-hand information about travel authors and their writing projects, travelogues in print and successful publications. In a letter to Mrs Gwatkin, Hannah More mentioned that Thomas Cadell had told her about 4,000 copies of Johnson's *Journey to the Hebrides* which had been sold during the first week after publication. The Bluestocking thought it was 'an agreeable work' and wished she could have conveyed the book to her friend.[145] More also documented the pre-publication discussion of *Journey* at Johnson's house, in which she had participated.[146] The amount of epistolary advice, comment and critical judgement about travel accounts augmented considerably in the summer and autumn periods when the Bluestockings left London for sea resorts, spa towns or their houses in the countryside, continuing to communicate with each other via post. In a letter to Montagu, Carter shared her impression of Henry Maundrell's *Journey from Aleppo*. Although first published in 1703, the book underwent several editions during the eighteenth century; it was read and discussed by the two friends in 1775. Carter wrote,

> I am glad to find you seem pleased with Maundrel's Travels,
> which, in spite of a bad style, and disagreeable manner, is,
> I think, a very useful and entertaining account. To have
> rendered it completely excellent, the author should have
> been capable of making such observations upon his subject,
> as those for which I am obliged to your letter. I believe you
> are right in thinking it might be dangerous to trust oneself
> amidst these sacred ruins.[147]

The Bluestockings were avid readers and their diaries and letters reveal their reading practices in general and how they read travelogues, in particular. Hamilton's diaries contain rich, untapped evidence of her 'most favorite amusement of Reading',[148] which was part of a daily pattern

---

[145] Roberts, *Memoirs*, vol. 1, p. 39. [146] Roberts, *Memoirs*, vol. 1, p. 49.

[147] *Letters from Mrs. Elizabeth Carter*, vol. 2, p. 337.

[148] HAM/2/14 1 September 1784.

of her activities. In them, Hamilton represented herself as an intellectually curious woman who tried not to be 'idle' and employed every spare minute to read a book. The young woman read at home – in her boudoir or drawing room and occasionally in bed; she read in a carriage and outdoors when she stayed in her friends' country houses. She read in the morning before breakfast, during the daytime between meetings and visits or in the evening when she stayed at home. Reading and writing were Hamilton's constant activities; numberless diary entries recorded her routine engagement with both of them. Here are her typical records: 'Read & wrote the Whole Morn[in]g.'; 'read & wrote went to bed at ½ past 12'; 'I read till one in the Morn[in]g.'; 'Staid at home all day – read & wrote'.[149] A series of passages from Hamilton's diaries testifies to the Bluestocking's practice of reading books during time-consuming hairdressing sessions, 'Betty dress'd my Hair & kept me near 2 hours to make me smart. I read during the time. . . . I generally read whilst my hair is dressing by w[ch] means that time is not so idle spent';[150] or 'as Betty generally is an hour & sometimes longer & as I read always, my hair dressing is never lost time';[151] and again, 'I am just risen from being under M[rs] Harmans (Bettys Sister) hands near 3 hours What a waste of time! – however I always read so I need not say that.'[152] Hamilton also contrived to unite work with reading, 'I dislike working when I am alone particularly when there is neither fancy nor taste in what I am doing therefore when it is necessary for me to employ myself in working I always have a book open before me & either refresh my memory or get something new.'[153] Hamilton's desire to read books was so strong that she could not deny herself the pleasure even when she suffered from eye inflammation, 'I stole an opportunity of scribbling in my Diary & reading a little as AM [Anna Maria] was not wth me.'[154] The young woman's friend Anna Maria Clarke had to 'spy' on Hamilton to prevent her from damaging her eyesight, and Hamilton complained that 'AM would not let me read or write.'[155] Later, she recorded, 'I employ'd myself till dinner time

---

[149] HAM/2/14 15, 16, 17, 20 July 1783. [150] HAM/2/9 25 March 1784.

[151] HAM/2/12 24 July 1784. [152] HAM/2/15 3 January 1785.

[153] HAM/2/15 20 January 1785. [154] HAM/2/14 29 August 1784.

[155] HAM/2/14 26 August 1784.

in doing trifling things that could not affect my Eyes – D[ea]ʳ AM came to me every now & then to spy whether I was reading or writing.'[156] Importantly, Hamilton was reading Cook's *Voyages* at that time.

Other Bluestockings' diaries and letters also contain snippets on their reading practices. In 1776, More confessed that 'in the midst of all the pomps and vanities' of London she studied 'like a dragon', writing a lot and reading four or five hours a day.[157] Her friend Eva Maria Garrick, who became the sole owner of the large book collection after her husband's death, shared Hannah More's love of reading. Describing their solitary stay at Hampton in winter, the Bluestocking noted that they 'read as much as any two doctors of either university'.[158] This simile indicates the intensity and amount of their reading and positions these women at the same intellectual level as male scholars. In *Thraliana*, for instance, Trale Piozzi contemplated some advantages of reading on the move and concluded that 'a Book is better than a Friend in a Carriage' as the noise that carriages always produced did not interfere with reading.[159] After her resignation from the court, Burney enjoyed the quiet and intellectually encouraging atmosphere of her father's house, 'We read together, write together, chat, compare notes, communicate projects, and diversify each other's employments. . . . I read more than I write. . . . The library or study, in which we constantly sit, supplies such delightful variety of food, that I have nothing to wish.'[160] Some Bluestockings had to limit their reading hours due to advanced age and health issues. Seventy-four-year-old Mary Delany did not cease reading books though she had to adopt a special reading regimen, 'I never read more (and seldom so much) as *two hours together*, but rest between, and chuse good prints for candle light.'[161] In a letter to her brother, Delany noted with satisfaction that the Duchess of Portland, at whose house in Bulstrode she spent six months annually for many years, shared her reading interests, 'we read and like the *same* books; we talk them over without interruption, we are fond of the *same* works; and the pleasures of these occupations are

[156] HAM/2/15 1 September 1784.   [157] Roberts, *Memoirs*, vol. 1, p. 71.

[158] Roberts, *Memoirs*, vol. 1, p. 167.   [159] Balderston, *Thraliana*, vol. 1, p. 461.

[160] D'Arblay, *Diary*, vol. 5, pp. 262–3.

[161] Llanover, *The Autobiography*, vol. 2, p. 50.

increased by participation.'[162] Delany's remark exemplifies eighteenth-century shared reading, the 'literary experience in which place, company, food, drink, and accessibility all play an important part'.[163]

In a letter to her great-niece Georgina Port, the celebrated friend and correspondent of Jonathan Swift expressed her thoughts on the benefits of reading:

> Reading will not only make you wise, but good in a serious way; and supply you with infinite entertainment in a pleasant way. Reading will open your mind to every ingenious *art* and *work*, and by observing how amiable a well informed person makes herself and how much esteem'd, it will raise your desire of being the same. I hope, you don't neglect your geography. . . . Pray tell me what book are you now reading?[164]

Delany gently cultivated Georgina's interest in reading travels, and one of her letters transcribed her conversation with the Princess Royal, 'The Princess Royal did me the honour to ask after you . . . 'what books you read?' . . . 'what books you liked?' I said you seem'd to like history and travels as far as you cou'd yet understand them.'[165] Delany herself was an avid reader of travel books, 'I have begun Mr Penant's tour thro' Scotland, and shall read till my eyes ache', she wrote to her niece once.[166] For Thrale Piozzi, the acquisition of geographical knowledge and regular reading of travels were an integral part of the programme which the Bluestocking designed for her daughters' intellectual improvement. She proudly noted that her 'second Daughter Susanna Arabella who will not be nine Years old till next May . . . has worked a Map of Europe, and has a comprehensive Knowledge of Geography that would amaze one.'[167] Thrale Piozzi read out

---

[162] Llanover, *The Autobiography*, vol. 2, p. 74. [163] Williams, *The Social Life*, p. 3.
[164] Llanover, *The Autobiography*, vol. 2, pp. 447–8.
[165] Llanover, *The Autobiography*, vol. 3, p. 71.
[166] Llanover, *The Autobiography*,., vol. 1, p. 411.
[167] Balderston, *Thraliana*, vol. 1, p. 361.

to her daughters the books which she 'could not force or perswade [sic] them to read for themselves', including 'some Travels through the well-known Parts of Europe'.[168]

Eighteenth-century travelogues were read out not only to children; the evidence suggests that this practice remained popular with the Bluestocking readers as well. Delany's letters give us an idea of how travelogues were read out in Bulstrode. In many cases, Delany used the pronoun 'we' when she recorded her reading; this indicates at least two constant members of the Bulstrode reading circle – she and the Duchess of Portland – though John Lightfoot, who spent many evenings there, seems to have been the third member. Other temporary members could have included many guests to Bulstrode. Mary Hamilton's records of reading out Coxe's travelogue during her stay there in 1783, which this section mentioned earlier, convincingly prove the point. In 1774, for instance, Delany informed John Dewes of reading Pennant's *Tour*, 'We have been very well amused with it; his acc[ts] may be depended upon, which gives one satisfaction.'[169] Two years later, Delany was more specific about their mode of collective reading, 'We have lately enjoy'd a very pleasing tranquility. Our last book (for we work and read in turns) was Mr. Pennant's last tour to Scotland.'[170] Reading out a travelogue was also documented by Burney who recorded how Cook's *Voyages* were read out at Norbury Park, 'Our mornings, if fine, are to ourselves . . . if bad, we assemble in the picture room. We have two books in public reading, Madame de Sévigné's Letters, and Cook's last Voyage. Mrs Locke reads the French, myself the English.'[171] Cook's voyages were also read out in the Clarges street; Hamilton noted, '[I] finish'd my Boxes – AM read to me in Cookes Voyages' and 'AM read to me till ½ past 10 in Cookes [sic] Voyages.'[172]

Although records of public reading are not rare, the analysis of the Bluestockings' diaries and letters suggests that in most cases silent reading of travels prevailed over social reading of the genre. Published frequently as

---

[168] Balderston, *Thraliana*, vol. 1, p. 591.

[169] Llanover, *The Autobiography*, vol. 2, p. 20.

[170] Llanover, *The Autobiography*, vol. 2, p. 282.

[171] D'Arblay, *Diary*, vol. 2, p. 322.   [172] HAM/2/14 26, 27 August 1784.

multivolume editions, contemporary travel accounts were supposed to be informative, encompass a broad range of subjects and be 'packed' with various data. The conventional generic requirements prescribed travel narrative to be emotionally neutral and devoid of much personal detail. Therefore, the following of travel texts during the reading-out sessions could have required concentration from the audience, making it a more intellectual than entertaining activity. Some travelogues addressed the specific subject matter. In her letter to Delany, Boscawen wrote, 'I was thinking of you last night, my dear madam, while I read a little book, entitled "An Extract from the Observations, made in a tour to Italy, by Chev. de la Condamine." These observations are chiefly *sur l'histoire naturelle*, fossils, metals, &c &c. While I perused this little book that came in my way, I said to it, "Mrs. Delany wou'd like you." ' [173]

Thrale Piozzi's letters to her daughter Queeney contain evidence on the writer's mode of active reading which indicates the intensive knowledge acquisition. She 'filled hundreds of volumes which passed through her hands with notes, comments, and stories'.[174] The Bluestocking acknowledged, 'I have a Trick of writing in the Margins of my Books, it is not a good Trick, but one longs to say something & cannot stop to take out the Thraliana.'[175] She read travelogues in the same way. Informing Queeney about Coxe's *Travels*, Thrale Piozzi noted, 'I worked thro' that huge Quarto (in my way of working) between 4 o'clock o'Monday Noon, and four o'Clock o' Wensday [sic] Noon.'[176] The passage, inter alia, is telling of the high velocity of Thrale Piozzi's reading. Hamilton, in her turn, copied extracts from travelogues in her commonplace book; there we find two extracts from Francis Carter's *Journey* and Pennant's *Tour*, indicated 'From Pennants Tour in Scotland 1769 3^d Ed: Quarto. Page 7'.[177] An episode of travelogue rereading, found in one of Delany's letters, signals the long 'reading life' of some eighteenth-century travelogues. She recommended 'Addison's Travels in Italy' which she thought to be 'concise, clear, informing, and written in a very agreeable style'. As an additional

---

[173] Llanover, *The Autobiography*, vol. 2, p. 52.   [174] Clifford, *Hester Lynch*, p. 449.
[175] Balderston, *Thraliana*, vol. 2, p. 780.
[176] Bloom and Bloom, *The Piozzi Letters*, vol. 1, p. 80.   [177] DDX/274/18.

argument, Delany mentioned that they – the Bulstrode reading circle – were reading it 'again'.[178]

The Bluestockings' reading records give an idea of the effect which contemporary travel accounts produced on them. In 1776, Boscawen was reading Pennant's travelogue borrowed from Delany. In a letter, she thanked her friend for the book, 'I must not be so ungratefull [sic] as to omit thanking you for Mr. Pennant, who entertains me very well sometimes, I will keep him a little longer.'[179] Later, writing back to Delany, who had permitted Boscawen not to send the book back, the Bluestocking hostess wrote, 'You are travelling with Mr. Pennant, you say – do you not then want yr volume again?'[180] What is indicative here is that Delany acknowledged that she had virtually journeyed with the author. In the same way, Carter followed Cook's voyages and wrote of 'the shore of a frozen ocean, surrounded by mountains of perennial snow' that her imagination might have drawn, and 'the howl of stormy winds, the bellowing of sea horses, and the growl of hungry bears', she might have heard while reading about the Arctic Circle.[181] Hannah More revealed her virtual travels with Gilpin while she was reading his *Observations*. In a letter to Walpole, which was sent from Montagu's estate in Sandleford, she admitted that the book had taught her to appreciate the beauty of the countryside, 'I have been an arrant stroller; amusing myself by sailing down the beautiful river Wye, looking at abbeys and castles, with Mr. Gilpin in my hand to teach me to criticize, and prominences, with all the cant of connoisseurship, and then to *subdue* my imagination, which had been not a little disordered with this enchanting scenery'.[182] Gilpin's travelogue gave Frances Burney great aesthetic pleasure and her diary reveals the writer's lively response to it, 'It is the most picturesque reading I ever met with: it shows me landscapes of every sort, with tints so bright and lively, I forget I am but reading, and

[178] Llanover, *The Autobiography*, vol. 1, p. 63. Delany recommended *Remarks on Several Parts of Italy, &c in the Years 1701, 1702, 1703* by Addison, first published in 1705.

[179] Llanover, *The Autobiography*, vol. 2, p. 257.

[180] Llanover, *The Autobiography*, vol. 2, pp. 262–3.

[181] *A Series of Letters*, vol. 4, pp. 345–6.   [182] Roberts, *Memoirs*, vol. 1, p. 319.

fancy I see them before me, coloured by the hand of Nature.'[183] Also, the reading of travelogues could function as a post-travel activity, which gave an opportunity to compare one's impressions of the place, which had already been seen, with the author's ideas of it and gain more knowledge about it. Delany recommended John Dewes to read one of Pennant's travelogues, 'which I think entertaining, and must be more so to you, who have explored some of its paths'.[184] Evidence suggests that the Bluestocking reader's imagination could be both activated and captivated by contemporary travel accounts to such an extent that they literally 'gulped' the books; the accomplished female readers either 'devoured' them, as Thrale Piozzi did, or read 'till my eyes ache', as Delany experienced.[185]

The Bluestockings' diaries and correspondence provide us with evidence on how they accessed books and, in particular, travelogues. They frequently borrowed books from their relations or fellow Bluestockings. Mary Hamilton complained that she could not afford to buy all the books that she wanted to read, 'After tea Mrs Walsingham shew'd a Book she has lately bought wch seems a curious & interesting work – I sh^{d} like to buy it but my pocket money wont allow of such indulgencies.'[186] Hamilton recorded that she borrowed books from her Bluestocking friends – Vesey, Garrick and Walsingham – and her extended family member, Lord Stormont, who had a large book collection. Burney also borrowed books from other Bluestockings. In 1786, she noted, 'My present book is Gilpin's description of the Lakes of Cumberland and Westmoreland. Mrs. Delany has lent it to me.'[187] Moreover, the writer borrowed books from her 'royal mistress', and not once.[188] Burney noted proudly that on one occasion Queen Charlotte gave her the keys 'to get, from her bookcase at her own house, Henry's History of England'.[189] Other courtiers also

[183] D'Arblay, *Diary*, vol. 3, p. 28.

[184] Llanover, *The Autobiography*, vol. 2, p. 282.

[185] Llanover, *The Autobiography*, vol. 1, p. 411.   [186] HAM/2/10 2 May 1784.

[187] D'Arblay, *Diary*, vol. 3, p. 28.

[188] D'Arblay, *Diary*, vol. 3, p. 234; vol. 4, pp. 108, 252.

[189] D'Arblay, *Diary*, vol. 5, p. 143.

supplied her with books; in 1786, Burney was reading Coxe's *Travels*, which had been sent by John Fisher.[190] The court chains of borrowers who became lenders could have included a member of the royal family and were rather long,

> To-day Mrs. Schwellenberg did me a real favour, and with real good nature; for she sent me the letters of my poor lost friends, Dr. Johnson and Mrs. Thrale, which she knew me to be almost pining to procure. The book belongs to the Bishop of Carlisle, who lent it to Mr. Turbulent, from whom it was again lent to the Queen, and so passed on to Mrs. Schwellenberg.[191]

To access travel accounts, the Bluestockings used circulating libraries, which on a par with subscription libraries, always had a choice of travel books to satisfy a high demand for the genre.[192] In the summer of 1789, Burney subscribed to the library in Weymouth 'which is not a bad one';[193] and later to 'the Saltram Library'.[194] Lady Herries informed Hamilton that she had borrowed Savary's travelogue from the library and advised her friend, who resided in Derbyshire at that time, to use the circulating library in the neighbourhood, 'Have you read Savary's letters sur l'Egypte? – If not do if you can meet with them for they will divert you both & have a great deal of information too – If you cannot get them in French perhaps the circulating Libraries will have them in English; – for I have had them from Hookham's.'[195] Sometimes, the Bluestockings informed their addressees about the third person who possessed the book which they advised to read. For instance, Delany suggested her niece borrow Addison's *Remarks* 'of Sir Charles Mordaunt'.[196] Delany actively sent travelogues to her relatives, of which she wrote in her letters, though it is difficult to trace whether she lent the books or sent them as gifts. For example, in 1773 she informed that 'as soon as Solander's travels are published, which will be the week after next',

---

[190] D'Arblay, *Diary*, vol. 3, p. 134. [191] D'Arblay, *Diary*, vol. 4, p. 15.

[192] Towsey, 'First Steps', 467, 476. [193] D'Arblay, *Diary*, vol. 5, p. 37.

[194] D'Arblay, *Diary*, vol. 5, p. 56. [195] HAM/1/17/86

[196] Llanover, *The Autobiography*, vol. 1, p. 63.

the book would be sent to her brother.[197] Three years later, she asked her niece if she had sent her 'the Russian Letters' by Vigor.[198] Despite the fact that book borrowing saved money, Carter preferred to have her own copies, 'My dear Miss Talbot often used to laugh at me, and affirm I never would read any books but my own; and, indeed, if it is a book that pleases me, I never can have any great enjoyment of it in the hurry which I always feel to return any thing I have borrowed.'[199] Although direct references concerning the purchase of travel books by the Bluestockings have not been traced so far, there is substantial indirect evidence that shows their activity in acquiring travel accounts, which Section 5 discusses in detail.

Thus, numerous reading records offer insights into the reading life of the Bluestocking women and demonstrate that they acquired knowledge of the world not only through interaction with the travellers and explorers who visited their gatherings; they speak of the Bluestockings' systematic engagement in the reading of travels. These women kept newly published travelogues on their radar; their conversation parties provided space for face-to-face discussion and critical judgement of recent publications. In the summer and autumn period, their discussions on books of the genre continued distantly – in epistolary form. Travel accounts were read silently and in a company for entertainment and knowledge mining. Travelogues were widely circulated – borrowed, lent and gifted. The Bluestockings displayed a lively interest in books on travels well into old age. In 1799, eighty-year-old Carter wrote to eighty-one-year-old Montagu about François Levaillant's travelogue on Africa, noting that his descriptions of travel were entertaining.[200] As we see, Montagu Pennington, who wrote about Carter's lack of interest in 'modern geography' (see the beginning of Section 2), considerably undervalued his aunt's knowledge of contemporary geographical discoveries and travels.

---

[197] Llanover, *The Autobiography*, vol. 1, p. 508.

[198] Llanover, *The Autobiography*, vol. 2, p. 217.

[199] *Letters from Mrs. Elizabeth Carter*, vol. 2, p. 236.

[200] *Letters from Mrs. Elizabeth Carter*, vol. 3, p. 354.

4 Writing Travel Accounts

> What stoic Traveller wou'd try
> A sterile soil, and parching sky,
> Or dare th' intemperate Northern zone,
> If what he saw must ne'er be known?
> For this he bids his home farewell;
> The joy of seeing is to tell.
> Trust me, he never wou'd have stirr'd,
> Were he forbid to speak a word;
> And Curiosity wou'd sleep,
> If her own secrets must be keep:
> The bliss of telling what is past,
> Becomes her rich reward at last.[201]

In a letter to William Parsons in 1787, the to-be author of *Observations* Thrale Piozzi mused on travel writing:

> I should be sorry however that you were to set out again o' Travelling; the End of Labour is Rest; and the intention of gleaning up Ideas in distant Regions, is only to benefit home by their Dispersion, or enable a Man to endure home by their Combination. If the last Flight don't answer – You must out once more – but resolving always at least to write your Travels: for no one should rob his native Country of those Talents, which owe their Cultivation to the Soil in which they were originally dropt.[202]

These lines chime with the epigraph of this section and illustrate the period's idea about the writing of travel as a commendable activity for both men and women and occupation from which the nation greatly benefited. Clare Brant

---

[201] More, 'The Bas Bleu', pp. 83–4.
[202] Bloom and Bloom, *The Piozzi Letters*, vol. 1, p. 228.

argues that 'writing was such an important part of eighteenth-century travelling because it visibly ordered experience.'[203] Manuscript travel texts could take on several forms – notes, sketches, letters, journals or their combination – and were incessantly produced by Britons who were on the move. Their family, friends and acquaintances voraciously read them. The reading audience could be lesser or wider, but they always waited impatiently for the next portion of information. As Zoë Kinsley acknowledges, a multiplicity of handwritten travel accounts 'attest to the thriving practice of writing and reading manuscript texts that coexisted alongside, and often interacted with, the tradition of print travel writing'.[204] The Bluestockings did not stay away from the nation's 'obsession' with travel writing in the Enlightenment era.

The members of the Bluestocking circle were well-travelled women in their own right. Montagu, Carter, Thrale Piozzi, Burney and Hamilton journeyed through the Continent; many more went on home tours. Frequently, the Bluestockings travelled in twos. In 1763, Montagu and Carter went on a continental journey; in autumn 1770, Chapone accompanied Montagu on her tour to Scotland from which she 'derived considerable pleasure and amusement'.[205] Burney travelled with Thrale Piozzi and her family to Brighton in 1779 and Bath in 1780; after her resignation from the court in 1791, the writer toured south-west England with Ann Ord. More collective tours had been planned but did not materialise for various reasons. In 1783, Hamilton and Anna Clarke were 'laying a scheme for going to Italy' and Clarke gave her friend lessons in Italian.[206] A year later, More, Garrick and Walsingham were preparing a journey to see the lakes of Cumberland; they informed several friends of it but abandoned the trip due to the illness of Walsingham's son.[207] Nevertheless, these records of unfulfilled travel projects testify to the Bluestockings' intellectual curiosity and

---

[203] C. Brant, *Eighteenth-Century Letters and British Culture* (Chippenham and Eastbourne: Palgrave Macmillan, 2010), p. 229.

[204] Kinsley, *Women Writing*, p. 55. [205] *The Posthumous Works*, vol. 2, p. 3.

[206] HAM/2/3.

[207] Roberts, *Memoirs*, vol.1, p. 390; D'Arblay, *Diary*, vol. 2, p. 352.

willingness to obtain new experiences, see unfamiliar surroundings and get acquainted with customs and manners of other people.

This section aims to demonstrate that the Bluestockings not only frequently conversed about travels and read travelogues, which Sections 2 and 3 discuss respectively, but they engaged in producing travel accounts as well. Section 4 argues that their output of travel texts, which is composed of letters written on the road (hereafter referred to as on-the-road letters), travel journals and Thrale Piozzi's *Observations*, should be considered the Bluestockings' contribution to the eighteenth-century corpus of travel texts and the period's cultural production. It added to geographical knowledge creation and dissemination, helped the authors to improve their literary style and indirectly encouraged the readership to adopt and pursue similar writing practices in future travels. By charting how these texts were received and circulated, this section illuminates their 'social life' within the Bluestocking circle and beyond.

The first group in the corpus of the Bluestocking-authored travel texts is presented by on-the-road letters which discussed travel itineraries and/or contained travel impressions as well as assessment of other societies.[208] They 'framed enquiry through description that acknowledged empirical obligations and the subjective basis of evaluation'.[209] During their four-month continental tour in 1763, both Montagu and Carter sent letters to their relations and friends including Boscawen, Vesey and Talbot. Carter's letters to Talbot are full of entertaining descriptions and reflections on the places the friends had visited and the people they had met.[210] Her addressee's return letters are no less interesting, as they contain evidence of how enthusiastic the readership's response to travel letters could be; the receiving was not a small event in itself. Talbot confessed to Carter that 'whenever your Letters come the day is marked with an agreeable incident – and that let me tell you is no small matter in days so uniform as our's [sic] at Lambeth in England.'[211] Letters from abroad could enhance the addressee's

---

[208] See, for example, E. Major, 'Feminity and National Identity: Elizabeth Montagu's Trip to France', *ELH*, 72.4 (2005), 908–18.

[209] Brant, *Eighteenth-Century Letters*, p. 245.

[210] Pennington, *Memoirs*, vol. 1, p. 251–376.　[211] *A Series of Letters*, vol. 3, p. 44.

status as a well-informed and well-connected person and serve as a medium through which the recipient could socialise with a wider circle of people. Talbot informed Carter of the audience's response to her letter which described bad roads and related their stay in Spa:

> Perdrigan is affronted at your mentioning the music of a cuckoo, when Spa it seems is famous for its nightingales. ... Mrs Francis, who was here two or three days ago ... is somewhat anxious to know whether the trimming is arrived bright and whole through so many disadventures. ... Charles Poyntz added that the very packing paper (a stronger texture than gauze) used to be shook to absolute powder in those rocky roads.[212]

Another comment is more revealing of how the Bluestockings' letters from abroad could boost the recipient's position in society:

> I am impatient for another Letter ... write about what you will, your Letters make me vastly important, et c'est a qui les aura le premier. As for Mrs Montagu's [letter], it would have heightened my importance beyond imagination, but in this point I was extremely honourable, resisted an almost irre-sistible temptation (for I actually did not show it to Lord Hardwicke, who came hither just as I had received the paquet ...) and by the very next Post sent it away to Mrs. Vesey.[213]

Talbot acknowledged that her mother regularly read Carter's continental letters, 'my mother, who loves variety, applauds you extremely for writing no more on one subject.'[214] The audience of these letters had become so wide that Carter reproached her friend for having circulated them so freely.

---

[212] *A Series of Letters*, vol. 3, pp. 44–5. [213] *A Series of Letters*, vol. 3, pp. 50–1.
[214] *A Series of Letters*, vol. 3, p. 51.

Talbot rejected Carter's idea of individual use of her letters and considered them as texts deserving wider audience:

> If I have been guilty of any sort of treachery in shewing a few of your Letters, I heartily beg your pardon. . . . In truth I do not see why one may not shew to proper persons such parts of Letters as are on general and indifferent subjects, where they will probably give pleasure to the reader, (and speaking of your's [sic]) improvement too, besides the credit they do the writer. To eat a whole fine peach one's-self, is greediness I never had an idea of, and I seriously looked on this as no more than helping my friends to a slice of the best I had.[215]

Due to lack of time, the Bluestockings, like other travellers, frequently duplicated their letters, slightly modifying them. Yet, this fact did not prevent their recipients from sharing and comparing their contents. In 1776, Boscawen, one of Montagu's addressees, informed Delany about 'a letter from Mrs. Montagu from Chaillot, very pleasant' and added that 'Mr. Burrows', Montagu's and Boscawen's mutual acquaintance, had also received a letter from her which, in the Bluestocking's opinion, had been 'still more entertaining'.[216]

Evidence from the Bluestockings' correspondence suggests that their letters written during travels were valued by their recipients for a number of reasons. They were cherished as a reliable source of information, particularly when it was impossible to obtain it otherwise. Responding to Montagu's letter from Scotland, Carter acknowledged,

> I am glad you were so well entertained by the conversation parties at Edinburgh. . . . I am much more inclined to envy your view of the relicks of the Caledonian monarchs.

---

[215] *A Series of Letters*, vol. 3, pp. 71–2.

[216] Llanover, *The Autobiography*, vol. 2, p. 263. John Burrows and his sisters were closely connected with the Bluestocking circle and visited Boscawen regularly.

> Indeed, the solemn antiquities of Holyrood House, have
> long been an object of curiosity to me, and I have harassed
> all my Scotch acquaintance with questions on that subject.
> None of them ever told me so much as you have done.[217]

Also, on-the-road letters had practical value and were useful in planning travel routes for the future as they contained much comment on sights, roads and hotel infrastructure. These letters acquired the value of friendship tokens as they testified to considerable time spent on writing. Besides, on-the-road letters invited those at home to virtually join the correspondent's journey. One of Talbot's letters to Carter illustrates the points:

> How much am I obliged to you, my dear Miss Carter, for
> stealing so many minutes from the amusing scenes around
> you, and from such companions as you have in this agree-
> able tour, to make me a partaker in your entertainments. . . .
> From hence you cannot expect nothing but thanks, for we
> untraveled folks have nothing to say that is worth
> reading. . . . Your chronologers at St. Omer's are delightful.
> With your guide to Lisle I am not a little angry. . . . I could
> gladly have accompanied you in your visits to the Niens.[218]

In the same vein, Carter appreciated Montagu's letters from Scotland and asked her friend for more, 'I shall be very glad to accompany you in your progress through the Highlands, whenever you are at leisure to give me that pleasure.'[219] On-the-road letters could evoke a range of positive emotions and sentimental feelings if the addressee happened to have visited the same place before. A telling comment is found in Carter's letter to Montagu in which she confessed how a friend's letter from Spa had evoked some pleasant memories,

---

[217] *Letters from Mrs. Elizabeth Carter*, vol. 1, p. 318.

[218] *A Series of Letters*, vol. 3, p. 38–41.

[219] *Letters from Mrs. Elizabeth Carter*, vol. 1, p. 321.

> I had a letter lately from Lady Dartrey, who is amused by
> the society at Spa. ... She is extremely charmed by the
> romantic scenery of the Sauveniere, to which she retires for
> two hours in the morning. Do you remember how much we
> delighted in this spot, and how we enjoyed the sitting there,
> till the rain drove us away.[220]

Hamilton's diaries offer more insight into how travel letters circulated through copying and reading them out. One of her commonplace books contains the copies of three long letters sent from a tour in Cumberland in 1779. They had been addressed to Charlotte Gunning and penned by John Lettice (1737–1832), the to-be author of *Letters on a Tour Through Various Parts of Scotland: in the Year 1792* (1794). In 1783, Hamilton brought her commonplace book to Bulstrode and Lettice's descriptions on Cumberland's natural beauties were read out to Delany and Bentinck, 'I read out of my Manuscript Book begun the letters from Mr Lettice to Miss Gunning an account of the lakes ... they work'd I read the 2nd Letter out of My Manuscript of the Lakes';[221] 'I read to them the 3^d of last letters of Mr Lettice's account of the Lakes of Cumberland.'[222] Hamilton did not give other detail but three sessions of 'social' reading must have provoked much discussion among the three women.

The second group in the corpus of travel texts authored by the Bluestockings is presented by manuscript travel journals. Unlike letters which were 'explicitly communicative', journals were 'annotative or introspective'.[223] Their production seems to have required more determination, writing discipline and a systematic approach from travellers who were expected to make day-to-day records pertaining to moving to or being in an unknown environment. Journal-writers showed preference for a more structured narrative through utilising a rigid framework of entries. Letters were more ephemeral – they could be lost, forgotten, stolen or destroyed – and the author lost control over his or her text after posting

---

[220] *Letters from Mrs. Elizabeth Carter*, vol. 3, p. 2.

[221] HAM/2/5 24 November 1783. [222] HAM/2/3 3 December 1783.

[223] Brant, *Eighteenth-Century Letters*, p. 229.

a letter. Journals were expected to enjoy a longer life and the author could exercise control over the narrative through revising and censoring it in the future. The choice of the journal format signals that travellers attached more value and significance to knowledge and experiences acquired far from home; while compiling journals, they could consider the possibility of circulating their texts, publishing in the future or preserving them for posterity.

Hamilton's manuscript travel journal resulted from her three-month tour to Spa in 1776. The young woman accompanied her friend Lady Dartrey and her family to the Continent; she found the journey improving for both body and mind. Not intended for publication, Hamilton's journal was designed to record the eventful itinerary of their journey through the Low Countries, to document new friendships and connections formed on the road and in Spa, and to make notes about the famous people she met on the tour.[224] The accomplished young woman perceived the journey as one of the key moments in her life, and the subsequent years proved that it was true. Hamilton discussed her experiences with her relations, friends and fellow Bluestockings. Apart from talking with Wraxall about numerous sights and relics seen on the road (discussed in Section 2), Hamilton documented two conversations with Bentinck and Delany about 'Spa, convents and some religious orders' at Bulstrode;[225] the Duchess of Portland also showed her 'a porte Folio of drawings views of Spa'.[226] Hamilton's lively interest in arts, history, antiquities as well as her perpetual 'quest for knowledge and advancement', which the Spa journal displays, testifies that she followed in the steps of young male counterparts on the Grand Tour.[227] The fact that the prolific diarist and letter writer preserved the journal among her papers till the end of life speaks of the importance and value attached to it.

---

[224] N. Voloshkova, 'The Dutiful Daughter: Mary Hamilton's Journal of her Visit to Spa in 1776' in P.J. Corfield and L. Hannan (eds.), *Hats, off! Changing Arts of Communication in the Eighteenth Century* (Paris: Honoré Champion Éditeur, 2017), pp. 99–105.

[225] HAM/2/3 30 November 1783. [226] HAM/2/6 16 December 1783.

[227] Voloshkova, 'The Dutiful Daughter', 108.

Other of Hamilton's records demonstrate that travel journals enjoyed a social life in the period; they provided evidence on how she received and read her male acquaintances' manuscript journals. In a diary entry of 1 July 1784, Hamilton noted, 'Rec[eive]^d a Note in French from Mr Richard Glover wth his Manuscript Journal written when in france [sic] & Italy'.[228] The following day she recorded how it was read out, 'After Supper AM [Anna Maria] read aloud some of Mr R. Glovers diary & I work'd.'[229] Or, for instance, Hamilton's friend and distant relation Francis Napier informed her of his 'Tour in the West Highlands' undertaken in 1783 and mentioned that he had 'made Memorands of every thing which I thought worth observing, intending to fabricate an immense Epistle for your leisure'.[230] In the same letter, Napier recommended Hamilton read Pennant's travelogue to get a better understanding of the places he had journeyed to, 'For a description of all these places I refer You to *Pennants Tour*'.[231] Later, Napier playfully 'threatened' Hamilton not to copy some extracts from his travel journal, 'To punish You for your sauciness, I have resolved not to copy one single Sheet of my Journal to the Highlands.'[232]

Thrale Piozzi was an ardent and prolific writer of manuscript travel journals; in various periods, she made written records on touring abroad and at home. The Bluestocking's love for travel writing had grown from her education and earlier writing practices. Recalling her youth, Thrale Piozzi acknowledged that she 'took up an odd Whim of writing in the Newspapers when She was a Girl of 14 and sent her letters slyly, no Friend suspecting her of such Employment'.[233] Writing became an inseparable part of her life; finding herself in an Italian town without pens at her disposal, she complained, 'Here is not a Pen in this place. . . . I am not only precluded by want of language from telling anybody else my Thoughts, but the having no Pen prevents me from telling them to myself.'[234] Thrale Piozzi's profound knowledge of geography was rooted in childhood, as 'Geography & Astronomy were her early Studies';[235] it also gleans from her book collection (see Section 5). The writer confessed that to engage accomplished

---

[228] HAM/2/11. [229] HAM/2/11. [230] HAM/1/20/83. [231] HAM/1/20/83.

[232] HAM/1/20/85. [233] Balderston, *Thraliana*, vol. 1, p. 322.

[234] Balderston, *Thraliana*, vol. 2, p. 620. [235] Balderston, *Thraliana*, vol. 2, p. 620.

foreigners into conversation and impress them with her knowledge, she discussed Cook's South Pacific expeditions with them, 'No Talk is more pleasing to cultivated Foreigners than some Conversation about Cook's Discoveries; I always turn to that page when I have a mind to make them like me.'[236]

Thrale Piozzi had adopted the habit of producing manuscript travel journals long before she set off with her second husband Gabriele Piozzi on 'so diverting a Drive round Europe', which lasted for two years and a half.[237] Her earlier journals were written during her tours in Wales in 1774 and France in 1775; Samuel Johnson accompanied Thrale Piozzi and her family on both journeys. In *Thraliana*, she recorded, 'When I went to France the Year after, I kept a Journal of all that passed, & so I did in the Welch Tour.'[238] The Welsh and French journals were not intended for publication;[239] apart from the writer's travel impressions, they contained much personal detail. Her French journal, for instance, documented how Thrale Piozzi arranged French classes for her daughter Queeney in Paris or took her for walks around the city. Although their stay in Paris was eventful in many ways, she found time to make records, 'I have stolen half an hour for my Journal & general Observations.'[240] In it, Thrale Piozzi documented the acquaintance with the renowned salonnière Anne-Marie du Bocage (1710–1802),[241] the author of *Letters on England*, and her impression of the travelogue.

Thrale Piozzi's later journal on touring Scotland, produced after the publication of her *Observations*, was written with a view of publishing in the future. Initially, the Bluestocking wanted to explore Ireland but had to abandon the idea, 'We talk of a Journey to Scotland this summer, I wish

---

[236] Balderston, *Thraliana*, vol. 2, p. 697. [237] Balderston, *Thraliana*, vol. 2, p. 678.

[238] Balderston, *Thraliana*, vol. 1, p. 114.

[239] They were published posthumously. See Tyson and Guppy, *The French Journals* and A.M. Broadley, *Doctor Johnson and Mrs Thrale: Including Mrs Thrale's Unpublished Journal of the Welsh Tour Made in 1774* (London and New York: John Lane, 1910).

[240] Tyson and Guppy, *The French Journals*, p. 93.

[241] Tyson and Guppy, *The French Journals*, pp. 91, 94, 102–3.

Ireland was to be our way home; but Cecilia & Piozzi both are afraid of the
Sea.'[242] Back home in December, Thrale Piozzi noted that they had
'returned ... after having run 1300 Post miles in Journeys about Great
Britain'[243] and added, 'I have written a little Acc^t of all I saw on my travels
in a Paper Book, so shall give myself no Trouble to say any thing of them in
this. When People press me to write my *Tour of our own Island* in good
Time!'[244] Like Montagu and Chapone, Thrale Piozzi was fascinated by
Scotland. She shared her impression of Edinburgh with the Reverend
Leonard Chappelow, 'my Fear was of a second hand London, but
Edinburgh is perhaps more like Paris or Potzdam [sic] than it is to anything
we possess in the Southern Parts of our Island ... we are going forward
through Glasgow to Loch Lomond, Inverary &c and I really now hope for
more Amusement in our Journey than once I counted on.'[245] Thrale
Piozzi's extensive travel abroad taught her to appreciate her country; she
thought that natural beauty of some places was undervalued, 'Why does
nobody ever talk of the Beauties of Exmouth? Devonshire is certainly the
Italy of England, & Derbyshire the Switzerland of it.'[246]

Thrale Piozzi went beyond the writing of travel in manuscript; she
converted her continental journals and *Thraliana*'s records, made between
1784 and 1787, into a travelogue and published it in 1789.[247] In doing this,
the Bluestocking tested her literary talent in another genre, strengthened
her 'status of authoritative cultural and social commentator'[248] and entered
a small group of British female travel writers in the late Georgian period.
For Thrale Piozzi, the writing of *Observations* presented a challenge: she
wanted in a non-offensive way to interpret the countries she had journeyed

[242] Balderston, *Thraliana*, vol. 2, p. 749. [243] Balderston, *Thraliana*, vol. 2, p. 749.

[244] Balderston, *Thraliana*, vol. 2,.p. 751.

[245] Bloom and Bloom, *The Piozzi Letters*, vol. 1, p. 303.

[246] Balderston, *Thraliana*, vol. 2, p. 718.

[247] H. Barrows, 'Introduction' in H.L. Piozzi, *Observations and Reflections Made in
     the Course of a Journey Through France, Italy and Germany* (Ann Arbor:
     University of Michigan Press; Rexdale: Ambassador Books Limited, 1967),
     p. xxiv.

[248] Turner, *British Travel Writers*, p. 1.

through and the people of other nations with whom she had come into contact, 'I will write my Travels & publish them – why not? 't will be difficult to content the Italians & the English but I'll try – & tis something to do.'[249] Through her travel narrative, Thrale Piozzi pursued two aims: her *observations* were to teach various facts that she had seen during her travels and her *reflections* were aimed at thinking about 'the significance that should be derived from the facts'.[250] In August 1788, the Bluestocking recorded completion of her 'Travel Book', which had been written in two months, though the text required further corrections.[251] In November, Thrale Piozzi noted with satisfaction, 'I *have* finished my Book and hope it will please the Publick – Individuals will be spiteful, but cannot hurt one much.'[252] Following the conventional generic requirements of the period, Thrale Piozzi frequently referred to earlier travelogues on Italy;[253] these references also indirectly attest to her extensive reading of travelogues. For instance, her description of La Capella St. Lorenzo in Florence mentions the impressions of the place given by Addison, Moore and the Earl of Cork.[254]

Notwithstanding a considerable number of travelogues on Italy, published by Britons before 1789, Thrale Piozzi's publication aroused a lively interest in the reading public. The author acknowledged, 'I think my Observations & Reflexions made in Italy &c have been upon the whole exceedingly well liked, & much read.'[255] Later, Thrale Piozzi's travelogue proved popular not only in England; it was also published in Ireland and its abridged German translation appeared in 1790.[256] On the whole, the travelogue received a positive critical response. A critic of the *London Review* thought that the book deserved readers' attention as it contained 'many sources of real entertainment'; at the same time, it was criticised for

[249] Balderston, *Thraliana*, vol. 2, p. 717.
[250] C.L. Batten, *Pleasurable Instruction: Form and Convention in Eighteenth-Century Travel Literature* (Los Angeles: University of California Press, 1978), p. 82.
[251] Balderston, *Thraliana*, vol. 2, p. 719. [252] Balderston, *Thraliana*, vol. 2, p. 720.
[253] Barrows, 'Introduction', xv.
[254] Piozzi, *Observations and Reflections*, pp. 138–9.
[255] Balderston, *Thraliana*, vol. 2, p. 751.
[256] Tyson and Guppy, 'Introduction' in *The French Journals*, 51.

'mean and vacant terms'. He praised the author for her openness towards new travel experience and ability to create a positive emotional atmosphere in the narrative, 'A lively good-humour attends upon her steps throughout the journey, and inspires a disposition to feel admiration and pleasure from every occurrence.'[257] In its turn, the *Critical Review* marked the author's attention to detail that allowed the audience to obtain a more nuanced panorama of Italy, 'From Mrs Piozzi, we receive much that other travellers have thought perhaps beneath their notice, but which fills up the picture of Italy, and is interesting to every one who would pursue nature in different paths.'[258]

Unsurprisingly, Thrale Piozzi's travel account was read and discussed in the Bluestocking circle. Despite the difficulty and tension in face-to-face communication with the author, which had been caused by her second marriage to Gabriele Piozzi, her fellow Bluestockings seem to have shown no hostility towards the travelogue. On 13 June 1789, Walpole informed Elizabeth Carter:

> You have therefore probably not looked into [Thrale Piozzi's] *Travels*. I, who have been almost six weeks lying on a couch, have gone through them. ... By the excessive vulgarisms so plentiful in these volumes, one might suppose the writer had never stirred out of the parish of St. Giles. Her Latin, French and Italian too, are so miserably spelt, that she had better have studied her own language before she floundered into other tongues. ... There are many indiscretions too in her work, of which she will perhaps be told, though B[aretti] is dead.[259]

[257] *The European Magazine, and London Review: Containing the Literature, ... by Philological Society of London*, vol. 16 (London: J. Sewell, 1789), p. 332.

[258] *The Critical Review: or, Annals of Literature. By a Society of Gentlemen*, vol. 68 (London: A. Hamilton, 1789), p. 105.

[259] Lewis, *Correspondence*, vol. 42, pp. 244–5.

Notwithstanding strong criticism of Thrale Piozzi's style expressed by Walpole, Carter formed her own opinion of the travel account. She appreciated *Observations*, though acknowledged some stylistic deficiencies of the narrative. Writing to Montagu in October 1789, Carter asked her friend if she had read the travelogue and wanted to learn her opinion of it:

> Have you, my dear friend, read Mrs Piozzi's travels? The book did not fall in my way till very lately. It was particularly pleasant to me during my illness, when I could not apply to any reading that required much attention. It is writ with spirit, acuteness, and much sensible observation. The style is sometimes elegant, sometimes colloquial and vulgar, and strangely careless in the grammatical part, which one should not expect from the writer's classical knowledge, which is very considerable, and which she applies very happily in many parts of her work. She sometimes puts me out of humour, by her being so vexatiously [sic] desultory. When she has led her readers to a building, which from its outside they are all impatience to enter, and wait for her to introduce them, away she whisks (do not you see her) and leaves them staring and wondering what is become of her. I felt this particularly with regard to the Cathedral of Milan, which was an object of great curiosity to me. One circumstance is highly to her honor, that she always mentions religion with the deepest reverence, and piety of expression. Do tell me if you have read this book, and whether you agree with me about it?[260]

As we see, Carter thought that Thrale Piozzi's profound knowledge of ancient languages and history gave her a big advantage. As a reader, the Bluestocking was dissatisfied with some 'inconsistency' of the text. Apparently, the smooth flow of narration was of great importance to the reader whose imagination was to be inspired by a travelogue.

---

[260] *Letters from Mrs. Elizabeth Carter*, vol. 3, p. 314.

In 1789, Burney asked her father if he had read Thrale Piozzi's travelogue and informed him that her 'Royal Mistress' had been reading the book
and promised to lend it to her.[261] Later, she recorded how Queen Charlotte
had read out some passages from *Observations*, 'The Queen is reading
Mrs. Piozzi's Tour to me, instead of my reading it to her. She loves reading
aloud, and in this work finds me an able commentator. How like herself,
how characteristic is every line! – Wild, entertaining, flighty, inconsistent,
and clever!'[262] The fact that the queen was reading out the travelogue to
Burney indicates at least three important things: a member of the royal
family was interested in the latest publications of the genre, social reading at
court could be egalitarian and the queen read out to the Bluestocking writer
the travelogue which was penned by the other Bluestocking writer. It was
not until the next year in April that Burney could get Thrale Piozzi's
Observations for silent reading, which she enjoyed thoroughly, 'To myself
I read Mrs. Piozzi's "Travels". The "Travels" are just like herself, abound-
ing in sallies of genius.'[263]

[261] D'Arblay, *Diary*, vol. 5, p. 36.   [262] D'Arblay, *Diary*, vol. 5, p. 38.
[263] D'Arblay, *Diary*, vol. 5, pp. 100–101.

5 Collecting Travel Books

> Lo! All in silence, all in order stand;
> And mighty folios first, a lordly band,
> Then quartos, their well-order'd ranks maintain,
> And light octavos fill a spacious plain;
> See yonder, ranged in more frequented rows,
> A humbler band of duodecimos;
> While undistinguish'd trifles swell the scene,
> The last new play and fritter'd magazine.[264]

The opening lines of Section 5 taken from George Crabbe's *Library* vividly convey an idea of an eighteenth-century book collection. In the year of its publication, the poem was in Thrale Piozzi's library, as Burney's diary record shows.[265] Two years later, Hamilton lent *Library* to Delany, 'Mr Sandford & his Brother . . . came in for a few Minutes I gave them – Mr Crabbes poem of the Library & Village to carry . . . to read to Mrs Delany.'[266] The epigraph sets the stage for the conversation on how the Bluestockings' interest in contemporary geographical knowledge and, particularly, travel accounts materialised in their home libraries. This section continues to explore the Bluestockings' engagement with travel accounts and discusses their ownership of books of the genre. Following Mark Towsey's convincing argument that catalogues of women's book collections can serve as 'basic indices of their reading lives',[267] it focuses on three private book collections possessed by Elizabeth Vesey, Eva Maria Garrick and Hester Thrale Piozzi. The section demonstrates that they owned a significant number of travel accounts and other publications such as geography books, travel guides, atlases, maps, prints and argues that

---

[264] G. Crabbe, 'The Library' in A. W. Ward (ed.), *Poems by George Crabbe*, vol. 1 (Cambridge: Cambridge University Press, 1905), p. 104.

[265] D'Arblay, *Diary*, vol. 2, p. 91.   [266] HAM/2/9.

[267] M. Towsey, 'Women as Readers and Writers' in C. Ingrassia (ed.), *The Cambridge Companion to Women's Writing in Britain, 1660–1789* (Cambridge: Cambridge University Press, 2015), p. 24.

the Bluestockings' accumulation of these materials was directly connected with the acquisition, creation and diffusion of contemporary geographical knowledge.

For the Bluestockings who constantly engaged in reading and writing, home library space was a meaningful place in both their homes and the houses of their relations, friends and acquaintances. A library, which usually occupied a separate room (sometimes rooms) in a house, symbolised a space saturated with wisdom and knowledge where everything was designated for intellectual pursuits. Long shelves of folios, octavos and duodecimos provided plenty of 'food' for the thinking mind and served as a window into the outer world. One of Bentick's and Delany's friends and attendees at the Bluestocking gatherings was Lady Bute, the daughter of the celebrated travel writer Mary Wortley Montagu and accomplished woman in her own right. Delany, who visited the Butes in their estate in Luton Hoo in 1774, was impressed by the magnificence of their home library and described it in a letter to her brother:

> You then go into the library, the dimensions of which I have been so stupid as not to remember. It is, in effect, three or five rooms, one very large one well-proportioned in the middle each end divided off by pillars, in which recesses are chimneys; and a large square room at each end, which, when the doors are thrown open, make it appear like one large room or gallery. I never saw so *magnificent* and *so pleasant* a library, extreamly [sic] well lighted, and nobly furnished with everything that can inform and entertain men of learning and virtü.[268]

In 1780, Hannah More admired the library in the country house of Lord and Lady Spencer in Wimbledon, 'we were quite at our ease, and strolled about, or sat in the library just as we liked. This last amused me much, for it was the Dss of Malborough's (old Sarah), and numbers of the books were presents to her from all the great authors of her time, whose names she

---

[268] Llanover, *The Autobiography*, vol. 2, p. 34.

had carefully written in the blank leaves.'[269] Thrale Piozzi's love of libraries gleans from her *Observations*, in which we find the descriptions of her visits to the famous libraries in Florence, Milan, Vienna and Dresden.[270]

The first book collection, which Section 5 analyses, is the Vesey library. Alongside Elizabeth Montagu, the Bluestocking hostess Elizabeth Vesey was known for her vibrant conversation parties acclaimed both in London and far beyond the metropolis; her house in Clarges Street operated as one of London's intellectual hubs of the day.[271] The contents of her vast book collection seemed to have been known to numerous friends and guests of the house. In the course of long learned conversations, certain books might have been shown, referred to or recommended, presented to the hospitable hostess or borrowed from her. During one of the gatherings at Clarges Street in 1784, as Hamilton recorded, 'Mrs Ord Mr Pepys & I look'd over some prints done from Drawings taken by Webber wch are publish'd wth Cooks Voyages just come in 4 Vol. Quarto – Government have granted £ 8000 towards this Publication & the Price of the Work is 4 Guineas & ½ … The Prints wch are bound up in a separate Vol: & are very well executed & the Subjects curious.'[272] The sales catalogue of the Vesey library informs us of a multivolume edition of Cook's *Voyages* in Vesey's possession;[273] this fact strongly suggests that her guests were looking through the book of prints from her library. On the whole, the catalogue provides invaluable information on the Bluestocking's intellectual interests and attests to their versatility; it indicates Vesey's extensive reading and testifies to 'her self-motivated lifelong commitment to the pursuit of knowledge and learning'.[274] The sales catalogue contains the information on the presence of the bookplates, autographs and inscriptions, which belonged to three family members; it allows us to trace the ownership within the

---

[269] Roberts, *Memoirs*, vol. 1, p. 174.

[270] Piozzi, *Observations*, pp. 139, 142–3, 327–8, 376–7, 384.

[271] Voloshkova, ' 'My friend' ', 96. [272] HAM/2/10.

[273] *The Library of Mrs. Elizabeth Vesey 1715–1791* (Newcastle-on-Tyne: William H. Robinson, 1926), p. 17.

[274] M.A. Stefanelli, 'Elizabeth Vesey and the Art of Educating Oneself, Between London and Lucan', *Studi Irlandesi: A Journal of Irish Studies*, 3 (2013), 323.

collection. All the book titles listed in the catalogue (hereafter referred to as books) have been divided into five groups: (1) the books owned by Elizabeth Vesey, (2) those belonging to her husband Agmondisham Vesey, (3) those possessed by his nephew and heir George Vesey, (4) those of shared ownership (with two family member's bookplates or autographs) and (5) the books without marks of ownership.

The books which bore Elizabeth Vesey's bookplate, autograph or inscription have been selected as those which belonged to the Bluestocking; they come from the first and, partly, the fourth groups. Further, two subgroups – travel accounts and other publications related to geography – have been identified; they are listed in Appendix 2. Out of 230 (100 per cent) books, which were owned by the Bluestocking, 15 books were identified as travelogues and 10 items as other publications related to geography, which constitute 6.52 per cent and 4.36 per cent respectively; the total number amounts to 25 items or 10.9 per cent. Appendix 2 shows that the travelogues accumulated by Vesey related the voyages round the world as well as travels in Europe, Asia, America, Africa and Australia; not a single female-authored travel account has been traced in her book collection so far. Three travelogues out of 15 related travels in Russia; they were penned by Hanway, Bell and Abbe Chappe D'Auteroche. The ownership of these books further strengthens the argument about the Bluestockings' interest in travel accounts on Russia (see Section 3). Vesey possessed four travelogues on journeys in Italy, which were published between 1760 and 1790; this fact may signal her long-lasting interest in the traditional Grand Tour destination. Also, Vesey owned four books on geography by Adams, Gordon, Harris and Wright; three of them were printed between 1730 and 1740, which suggests Vesey's early possession of them.

The second private book collection that Section 5 focuses on is the private library which was owned by the celebrated actor and theatrical manager David Garrick. After his death, it was inherited by his wife Eva Maria Garrick, who not only preserved but also added to the collection during her widowhood. By the time of the sale in 1823, the library was composed of more than 3,000 books (many in multivolume sets);[275] it was

---

[275] *A catalogue of the Library, splendid books of prints, poetical and historical tracts, of David Garrick, Esq removed from his villa at Hampton, and house on the Adelphi*

particularly rich in rare British and foreign editions and included many contemporary presentation copies to David Garrick. In late Georgian Britain, book lending became 'something of a social imperative in the polite culture', and family libraries frequently operated as a 'practical resource for the wider community'.[276] Evidence from the Bluestockings' diaries and correspondence suggests that the Garrick library performed the same function in the Bluestocking circle; at least two Bluestockings documented that they benefitted by borrowing books from it. Garrick's close friend Hannah More stayed long periods at both houses – the city house and Hampton villa; the writer used the library on a regular basis (see Section 3). In a letter to Boscawen, More noted, 'Talking of long evenings and retreats, I took it into my head during my seclusion at Hampton last year to read through a shelf of books as they came to hand, without any choice or selection.'[277] Eva Maria Garrick lent books to Mary Hamilton who could not afford to buy them in the numbers she had wished; the young woman left evidence of the library catalogue circulation. In September 1784, Garrick sent Hamilton 'the Catalogue of her late Husbands library (the one at the Adelphi) to chuse [sic] out any book I wish'd to read'.[278] The following day the young woman 'look'd over the Catalogue chose a few Books – wrote a long Note to Mrs Garrick & return'd the Catalogue *early* in the Morn[in]g'.[279] Regretfully, Hamilton did not note what her reading choice was but her correspondence encloses a letter from Garrick in which she apologized for having sent the wrong book to Hamilton.[280] Futhermore, one of Hamilton's diaries mentions the inscription the books in the collection contained, 'In the Books in Garricks Library's at Hampton & London The following lines were printed & pasted on ye inside of the cover. La premiere chose qu'on doit faire quand on a emprunté un Livre c'est de le lire afin de pouvoir le render plütôt'.[281]

Terrace, with the modern works added thereto by Mrs Garrick, which will be Sold by Auction, by Mr. Saunders at his Great Room, 'The Poets' Gallery,' No. 39, Fleet Street, on Wednesday, April 23d, 1823.

[276] Towsey, ' "I can't resist"', 210. [277] Roberts, *Memoirs*, vol. 1, p. 333.

[278] HAM/2/14 11 September 1784. [279] HAM/2/14 12 September 1784.

[280] HAM/1/6/6/1. [281] DDX 274/18.

The analysis of the library has shown that Eva Maria Garrick accumulated a significant number of travel accounts and other printed publications related to geography. Appendix 3 lists those which were published between 1779 and 1822 and, consequently, acquired in that period; it means that they were accumulated by Garrick after her husband's death in January 1779. She purchased at least 169 books, including 25 travelogues and 6 items identified as other materials related to geography. Out of 127 (100 per cent) books, which were acquired by Garrick between 1779 and 1799, 17 books were identified as travelogues and 6 items as related to geography, which constitute 13.39 per cent and 4.72 per cent respectively. The total number amounts to 23 items or 18.11 per cent. Appendix 3 demonstrates that the travelogues acquired by Garrick related travels in Europe, Asia, America and Africa. She seems not to have been much interested in books on travels at home, only *Letters from Mountains* (1806) penned by Anne Grant has been identified so far. Importantly, Garrick possessed three of the four travelogues which were the most popular with the Bluestockings between 1780 and 1790 (see Section 3): Bruce's *Travels*, Coxe's *Travels* and Thrale Piozzi's *Observations*. Four female-authored travelogues penned by Montagu, Thrale Piozzi, Grant and Plumtree were traced in Garrick's possession.

Thrale Piozzi's library was an intellectual centre of Streatham Park. In her *Diary and Letters*, Burney recorded the days when she set off for 'book hunting'[282] or just 'stayed in the library reading'.[283] Thrale Piozzi's love for travel and reading of travels materialised in her private book collection, which contained a considerable number of travelogues and other printed materials related to geography. Her library was sold in two auctions in 1816 and 1823.[284] Appendix 4 lists travel books and other materials related to

---

[282] D'Arblay, *Diary*, vol. 1, p. 82. [283] D'Arblay, *Diary*, vol. 2, p. 80.

[284] 'A Catalogue of the Excellent and Genuine Household Furniture . . . Also, the Extensive and Well-Selected Library, Containing near 3000 volumes . . . of Mrs. Piozzi . . . which will be Sold by Auction, by Mr. Squibb, on the Premises, on Wednesday the 8th of May' in *Sale Catalogues of the libraries of Samuel Johnson, Hester Lynch Thrale (Mrs. Piozzi) and James Boswell* (New Castle, Delaware, 1993), pp. 47–139; 'Catalogue of the Library, Pictures, Prints, Coins, Plate, China, and other Valuable Curiosities, the Property of Mrs Hester Lynch

geography which have been selected from two respective sales catalogues. Appendix 5 contains a list of books on travels and geography selected from Thrale Piozzi's manuscript inventory. Written in her hand and entitled *Catalogue of Books at Brynbella 18 Oc^tr 1806*,[285] the inventory lists 74 items on the subject and contains those books which were later sold at the auctions. Moreover, the manuscript gives an idea of Thrale Piozzi's mode of recording the book titles in an abridged form which indicates how well she knew her collection. The 1816 catalogue provisionally lists 15 travelogues and 6 items related to geography. It is impossible to trace the precise number as the catalogue frequently mentions a group or groups of books. The 1823 catalogue is more informative and Section 5 focuses on the evidence which comes from it. Out of 650 (100 per cent) books listed in the catalogue, 47 were identified as travelogues and 35 were identified as other printed materials related to geography, which constitute 7.23 per cent and 5.38 per cent, respectively. Taken together, they signal that the total number amounts to 82 items, which represents 12.61 per cent. The travelogues in the collection covered travel in all the parts of the world; particularly numerous were those on continental journeys. Thrale Piozzi owned all the travel accounts on Italy, France, Germany and Switzerland which she had mentioned in her *Observations*.

In the course of the comparative analysis of all travelogues owned by Vesey, Garrick and Thrale Piozzi. we have not traced any book or books which can serve as a 'meeting place' of three collections. Yet, ten travel accounts have been identified as common for two collections, nine of them related travels in Europe. Both Vesey's and Thrale Piozzi's libraries contained the travelogues authored by Baretti, Bougainville, Brydone, Boswell, Cook and Johnson. Both Garrick's and Thrale Piozzi's collections enclosed the travelogues penned by Moore, Montagu, Coxe and Piozzi. On the whole, the ownership of non-fiction travel accounts attests to the popularity

Piozzi, deceased, to be sold by Auction' in *Sale Catalogues of the libraries of Samuel Jonson, Hester Lynch Trale (Mrs. Piozzi) and James Boswell* (New Castle, Delaware, 1993), pp. 141–212.

[285] Hester Lynch Piozzi, Catalogue of the Books at Brynbella, 1806–1813. Thrale-Piozzi Manuscripts. University of Manchester Library. GB 133 Eng MS 612.

of the genre with the Bluestockings; the presence of other publications such as geography books, travel guides, atlases as well as maps and prints further strengthens the argument about their thorough geographical knowledge. Those Bluestockings who could afford to purchase many books accumulated a significant number of contemporary travelogues and shared them with other fellow Bluestockings. Evidence revealed in the catalogues, diaries and correspondence gives sufficient grounds for the argument that the Bluestockings' ownership of the printed materials related to geography was directly connected with their acquisition, production and diffusion of current geographical knowledge.

This Element completes the analysis of the Bluestockings' engagement with travel accounts with an anecdote that Thrale Piozzi had heard from one of her friends and later recorded in *Thraliana*. He told her that while 'sorting & classing a Friends Library, he had found *Mall Flanders* among the books of Geography – the owner thought it was Moll's [cartographer Herman Moll] Maps of Flanders no manner of doubt.'[286] This study has attempted to show that such a thing could never have occurred to the Bluestockings who had a profound knowledge of geography, owned many travel books and other materials on geography in their private libraries, interacted with the eminent travel writers and explorers of the day; their drawing rooms provided a setting for learned conversations on travel and exploration. These women were voracious readers of contemporary travelogues and penned their own travel texts: on-the-road letters, travel journals and a travelogue. In doing this, they took an active part in the period's cultural production and geographical knowledge diffusion. The author of the Element hopes that more evidence on the Bluestockings' reading of travel accounts as well as books on history, religion, science and gardening will be revealed and examined by researchers in the future.

---

[286] *Thraliana*, vol. 1, p. 221.

Appendix 1
The Bluestockings' Reading of Travelogues

This appendix reconstructs the Bluestockings' reading of travel accounts in the period between 1760 and 1799 by offering two lists. The first list includes the travelogues selected from the Bluestockings' diaries and correspondence and identified as definitely read by them. The data are organised in decades to demonstrate the correlation between the publication date and the year when the travelogues were read and discussed. It also lists the travel accounts which Thrale Piozzi referred to in her *Observations*. They were included in the 1780s period when both her continental travel was undertaken and the travelogue was written and published. The first list also includes Smith's travel account with Thrale Piozzi's MS notes, which the 1823 sale catalogue mentioned. The second list in this appendix represents the travelogues which were possibly read by the Bluestockings; references to them appear in their letters, diaries and marginalia.

Travel Books Definitely Read
by the Bluestockings
1760–1769

Addison, Joseph, *Remarks on Several Parts of Italy, &c in the Years 1701, 1702, 1703* (first pub. 1705), read by Delany in 1763; referred to in Thrale Piozzi's *Observations*

Montagu, Lady Mary Wortley, *The Turkish Embassy Letters* (1763), read by Talbot in 1763

1770–1779

Carter, Francis, *A Journey from Gibraltar to Malaga* (1777), read by Hamilton

Condamine, Chev. de le, *An Extract from the Observations made in a Tour through Italy* (1768), read by Boscawen in 1774

Du Bocage, Anne-Marie, *Lettres sur l'Angleterre et la Hollande* (French edition in 1762, English edition in 1770), read by Thrale Piozzi in Paris in 1775

Johnson, Samuel, *A Journey to the Western Islands of Scotland* (1775), read by More

Hawkesworth, John, *An Account of the Voyages* (1773), read by Chapone in 1773

Maundrell, Henry, *Journey from Aleppo to Jerusalem at Easter A.D. 1697* (first pub. 1703), read by Carter and Montagu in 1775

Pennant, Thomas, *A Tour in Scotland in 1769* (1771), read by Delany in 1772; read by Hamilton

Pennant, Thomas, *A Tour to Scotland, and Voyage to the Hebrides 1772* (1774), read by Delany, Bentinck, Boscawen in 1776

[Vigor, Jane], *Letters from a Lady who resided some years in Russia, to her friend in England; with historical notes* (1776), read by Delany in 1776

1780–1789

Boswell, James, *The Journal of a Tour to the Hebrides, with Samuel Johnson* (1785), read by Boscawen and Herries in 1785

Brydone, Patrick, *A Tour through Sicily and Malta* (1773), referred to in Thrale Piozzi's *Observations*

[Cook, James; King, James], *A Voyage to the Pacific Ocean* (1784), read by Carter, Burney, Hamilton in 1784

Coxe, William, *Travels into Poland, Russia, Sweden, and Denmark* (1784), read by Thrale Piozzi, Hamilton, Delany, Bentinck, Montagu, Carter in 1784; by Burney in 1786

Craven, Elizabeth, *A Journey Through the Crimea to Constantinople* (1789), read by Thrale Piozzi in 1789

Earl of Corke and Orrery, John, *Letters from Italy, in the Years 1754 and 1755* (1774), referred to in Thrale Piozzi's *Observations*

Gilpin, William *Observations on the River Wye* (1782), read by Delany, Bentinck, Hamilton in 1781–4

Gilpin, William *Observations, Relative Chiefly to Picturesque Beauty, Made in the Year 1772* (1786), read by Burney in 1786

Gilpin, William *Observations, Relative Chiefly to Picturesque Beauty, Made in the Year 1776* (1789), read by More in 1789

Lunardi (V.) *Aerial Voyage* (1784), read by Hamilton in 1784

[Miller, Anna], *Letters from Italy, describing the manners, customs, &c in the year 1770–1, to a friend residing in France* (1776), referred to in Thrale Piozzi's *Observations*

Moore, John, *A View of Society and Manners in France, Switzerland and Germany* (1779), referred to in Thrale Piozzi's *Observations*

Moore, John, *A View of Society and Manners in Italy* (1781), referred to in Thrale Piozzi's *Observations*

Piozzi, Hester Lynch, *Observations and Reflections* (1789), read by Carter in 1789; by Burney in 1790

Savary, Claude-Étiene, *Lettres sur l'Égypte* (1786), read by Herries in 1786

Sherlock, Martin, *Letters from an English Traveller* (1780), referred to in Thrale Piozzi's *Observations*

Smollett, Tobias, *Travels through France and Italy* (1766), referred to in Thrale Piozzi's *Observations*

Sharp, Samuel, *Letters from Italy, Describing the Customs and Manners of the Country* (1766), referred to in Thrale Piozzi's *Observations*

Tournefort, *Joseph Pitton de, Relation d'un voyage du Levant* (Fr. 1717, Eng. 1741), referred to in Thrale Piozzi's *Observations*

Ulloa, Antonio de, *Relación Histórica del Viaje a la América Meridional* (1748), referred to in Thrale Piozzi's *Observations*

1790–1799

Blainville, H. de, *Travels through Holland … Translated from French* (1743), read by Thralle Piozzi and discussed in *Thraliana* in 1794

Bruce, James, *Travels to discover the Source of the Nile* (1790), read by More, Burney, Piozzi in 1790

Gray, Robert, *Letters during the Course of a Tour through Germany, Switzerland and Italy* (1794), read by Thrale Piozzi

Smith, Sir James Edward, *A Sketch of Tour on the Continent in the Years 1786 and 1787* (1793), contains Thrale Piozzi's MS notes

Vaillant, Francois le, *Travels into the Interior Parts of Africa by the way of the Cape of Good Hope in the Year 1780*, transl. from French (1790), read by Thrale Piozzi in 1791, Carter in 1799

Travel Books Possibly Read by the Bluestockings

Bell, John, *Travels from St. Petersburgh in Russia, to Diverse Parts of Asia* (first pub. 1763), marginalia in Hamilton's diary

Boswell, James, *An Account of Corsica, the Journal of a Tour to That Island* (1768), mentioned by Delany in 1779, Thrale Piozzi in 1779

Byron, John, *The Narrative of the Honourable John Byron (Commodore in a Late Expedition round the World) Containing an Account . . .* (1768), mentioned by Thrale Piozzi in 1790

Colben, Peter, *The Present State of the Cape of the Good Hope* (1731), mentioned by Thrale Piozzi in 1791

[Hentzner, Paul], *A Journey into England by Paul Hentzner in the Year MDXCVIII* (1757), marginalia in Hamilton's diary

Thicknesse, Philip, *A Year's Journey Through France and Part of Spain* (1777), mentioned by Carter in 1779

Wraxall, Nathaniel, *Cursory Remarks Made in a Tour Through Some of the Northern Parts of Europe* (1775), mentioned by Hamilton in 1776

Appendix 2
Travel Accounts and Printed Materials Related to Geography Owned by Elizabeth Vesey

This appendix lists the travelogues and printed materials related to geography which have been identified as owned by Elizabeth Vesey. The abridged book titles are given in the order they appear in the sale catalogue.

Travel Accounts

La Condamine (C.M. de) *Relation Abregee d'un Voyage*, 1745.

Lockman (John) *Travels of the Jesuits*, 1743.

Baretti (Giuseppe Marc Antonio) *An Account of the Manners and Customs of Italy*, 1788.

Bell (John) *Travels from St. Petersburg in Russia*, 1763

Boswell (James) *An Account of Corsica*, 1768

Bougainville (Louis de) *Voyage round the World, 1666–69*, 1772

Brydone (P.) *Tour through Sicily and Malta*, 1773

Chappe D'Auteroche (Abbe) *Journey into Siberia*, 1770

Cook (Captain James) *Three Voyages Round the World*, 1773–85

Forster (J.R.) *Travels through Sicily, part of Italy, and a Tour through Egypt*, 1773

Gedoyn (Abbe) *Pausanian, ou Voyage Historique de la Grece*, 1731

Hanway (Jonas, Merchant) *An Historical Account of the British Trade over the Caspian Sea*, 1753

Johnson (Samuel) *A Journey to the Western Islands of Scotland*, 1775

Norden (F.L., Capt. of the Danish Navy) *Travels in Egypt and Nubia*, 1757

Tournefort (Pitton de) *Relation d'un Voyage du Levant*, 1727

Printed Materials Related to Geography

Adams (George) *A Treatise describing the Construction and Use of New Celestial and Terrestrial Globes*, 1766

Colden (C.) *History of the Five Indian Nations of Canada*, 1755

Raynal (Abbe) *Histoire Philosophique et Politique des Etablissements et du Commerce des Europeens dans les deux Indes*, 1772

Gordon (Pat.) *Geography Anatomiz'd; or, the Geographical Grammar . . . Folding Maps*, 1730

Burke (Edmund) *An Account of the European Settlements in America*, 1760

Harris (Joseph) *Description and Use of the Globes and the Orrery*, 1738

Ockley (S.) *The History of the Saracens*, 1718

Letters concerning the Present State of Poland, 1773

Compleat History of the Turks, 755 to 1718, 1719

Wright (Thomas of the City of Durham) *The Use of Globes*, 1740

Appendix 3
Travel Accounts and Printed Materials Related to Geography Acquired by Eva Maria Garrick between 1779 and 1822

This appendix presents a list of the items selected from the sale catalogue of the Garrick library. It includes the travelogues and printed materials on geography which were published in the period between 1779 and 1822 and acquired by Eva Maria Garrick after David Garrick's death in January 1779.

Travel Accounts

Bowdler's (Thomas) *Letters from Holland*, 1788

Bruce's (J.) *Travels to discover the Source of the Nile*, 5 vols., plates, wanting vol. 1, 1790

Coxe's (W.) *Travels in Switzerland*, 3 vols., map, 1789

Coxe's (W.) *Travels in Poland, Russia, Sweden and Denmark*, 4 vols., maps and plates, 1787

Coxe's (W.) *Account of the Russian Discoveries*, maps, 1787

Dutens *Mémoires d'un Voyageur qui se repose*, 3 tom, 1806

Eddis's (W.) *Letters from America*, 1792

Francklin's (W.) *Tour from Bengal to Persia*, 1790

Kotzebue's (A. Von) *Travels from Berlin to Paris*, 3 vols., 1806

La Harpe Abregé de l'Histoire Générale des Voyages, 1780

[Anne Grant] *Letters from the Mountains*, 1806

Lunardi's (V.) *AErial Voyage, port. By Bartolozzi*, 1784

Mackenzie's (Sir G.S.) *Travels in the Island of Iceland, coloured* plates, Edinb. 1811

Moreir's (J.) *Journey through Persia, Armenia and Asia Minor to Constantinople, map and* plates, 1812

Murphy's (James) *Travels in Portugal*, large paper, *plates*, 1795

Moore's (Dr John) *View of Society and Manners in Italy*, 2 vols., *neat*, 1783.

Moore's (Dr John) *View of Society and Manners in France, Switzerland, and Germany*, 2 vols., *neat*, 1783

Montagu's (Lady M.W.) *Works*, 1803

Park's (Mungo) *Travels in the Interior Districts of Africa*, *maps and plates*, 1807

Piozzi's (H.L.) *Journey through France, Italy and Germany*, 2 vols., 1789

Plumtree's [Miss] *Residence in France*, 1797

Staunton's (Sir Geo.) *Authentic Account of Earl Macartney's Embassy to China*, 2 vols., *plates and folio volume of maps and plates*, 1791

Stedman's *Narrative of an Expedition to Surinam*, 2 vols., *plates*, 1796

Wilson's (Henry) *Account of the Pelew Islands*, by Keate, large paper, *map*, 1788

Yorke's (H.R.) *Letters from France, in 1802*, 2 vols., 1804

Printed Materials Related to Geography

Historical Disquisition concerning India, 1791

Lysons's (Danl.) *Historical Account of the Environs of London and Middlesex Parishes*, 5 vols., *numerous plates*, 1792–1800

Paterson's (Danl.) *Roads in England and Wales*, 1784

Paterson's (Danl.) *Book of Roads*, 1792

Trusler's (John) *Habitable World Described*, 20 vols. in nos, *early impressions of the plates*, wanting nos 6, 8, 41, 69, 70 and 71, 1781 &c

Wraxall's (N.V.) *Memoirs of the Northern Courts of Europe*, 2 vols., 1799

Appendix 4
Travel Accounts and Printed Materials Related to Geography in Thrale Piozzi's Library

Travel Accounts (the 1816 Sale Catalogue)

Nugent's Tour, 4 [vols.]
Viaje de Espana, eight odd vols.
Baretti on Italy, 2 [vols.]
Tour to Malta, 2 [vols.]
Wraxall's Tour
Boswell's Account of Corsica
Piozzi's Journeys
Voyage de Bougainville, Paris, 1771
Hawkesworth's Voyages, 3 vols., Lond. 1773
Young's Tour in Ireland, Lond. 1780
Chandler's Travels in Asia Minor, 2 vols., Lond. 1776
Bougainville's Voyage, translated by Forster, Lond. 1772
Baretti's Travels from London to Genoa, 2 vols., Lond. 1770
De Blainville's Travels, 3 vols. Lond. 1757
Dr Brown's Travels, Lond. 1687

Printed Materials Related to Geography (the 1816 Sale Catalogue)

Descrizione del Vaticano
Nature Delineated, 4 [vols.]
Campbell's Survey of Great Britain, 2 vols.
Borlase's Scilly Islands, Oxford, 1756
Borlase's Antiquities of Cornwall, Oxford, 1754
Moll's Atlas, with MS. Index

Travel Accounts (the 1823 Sale Catalogue)

Smollet's Travels in France, 2 vol[s]., 1778

Cook's Voyages, abridged, cuts, 1788

H.M. Williams' Letters from France, 2 vol[s]., 1790

H.M. Williams' Sketch of the Politics of France, &c 2 vol[s]., 1795

Lady M. Montagu's Travels in Europe, &c, 2 vol[s]., 1778

Dupaty's Letters from Italy, 4 vol[s]., 1789

Potoni's Travels to Buenos Ayres, plates, 1806

Visit to Paris, 1814, plates, 1814

Paris as it was, and as it is, 2 vol[s]., 1803

Voyage Pittoresque de Paris, avec plances, Par., 1770

Patin Voyage en Angleterre, &c planches, 1695

Maundrel's Journey from Aleppo to Damascus, plates, 1786

Moore's View of Society in France, &c, 2 vol[s]., 1793

Stark's Letters from Italy, 2 vol[s]., 1800

Coxe's Sketches of Switzerland, 1799

Letters on the State of Holland, 1773

Smith's Tour on the Continent, 3 vol[s]., MS notes 1793

Bradbury's Travels into the Interior of America, 1817

Tooke's View of the Russian Empire, 3 vol[s]., 1800

Cooke's First Voyage, plates, 1775

Barrow's Voyage into the Arctic Regions, 1818

Hooker's Tour in Iceland, coloured plates. This book was not published for sale, 1811

Grantz' History of Greenland, 2 vol[s]., plates, 1772

Vaillant's Travels to the Cape of Good Hope, 2 vol[s]., plates, 1790

Anbury's Travels in the Interior of America, 2 vol[s]., plates, 1789

Letters from Barbary, &c, 2 vol[s]., 1788

Semple's Journey in Spain, 2 vol[s]., 1808

Rogers' Account of North America, 1765

Phillips' Morning Walk from London to Kew, 1807

Murray's Beauties of Scotland, 1799

Anderson's British Embassy to China, 1795

Jackson's Account of the Empire of Morocco, and District of Suse, 1809

Browne's Travels in Africa, Egypt, and Syria, plates, 1806. Very interesting MS account at the commencement with other notes.

Walpole 's Memoirs of Turkey, plates, 1817

Anson's Voyage Round the World, plates, 1767

Sandy's Travels in Turkey, Greece, &c, 50 plates, 1673

Herbert's Travels in Africa, Asia, &c, many plates, 1638

Wheeler's Journey into Greece, many plates, 1682

Wicquefort's Ambassador's Travels, 1720

Cook's Collection of Voyages, many plates, 1786

[Johnson] A Journey to the Western Isles of Scotland, a presentation copy . . ., 1785

[Johnson] *A Diary of a Journey into North Wales*, 1816

Lobo's Voyage to Abyssinia, 8 vo., 1735

Observations and Reflections in a Journey through France, Italy, &c, by L. H. Piozzi 2 vol[s]., 8 vo., 1789

Boswell's Life of Johnson and Tour to Hebrides, 8th Edition, 5 vol[s]., 1816

Boswell's Tour to the Hebrides, 1785

Printed Materials Related to Geography (the 1823 Sale Catalogue)

Burnett's Theory of the Earth, 2 vol[s]., 1722. (Learned Marginal MS notes)

Whiston's Theory of the Earth and Astronomy, 2 vol[s]., MS notes, 1738

Lettere Diverse di Gasp. Gozzi (MS notes)

Harris' Astronomy and Geography, 2 vol[s]., 1729

Picture of Paris, plates, 1814

[Henry Coxe] Picture of Italy, plates, 1815

D'Anville Ancient Geography, fine engravings, 1799

Verona Illustra, 2 tom con fig. Ver., 1771

Dictionnaire Geographique, 2 tom, Brux., 1792

Colden's Five Nations of Canada, 1747

Fowler's Account of the Hurricanes and Earthquakes in the West Indies, 1781

Manby's Beauties of Clifton, plates, 1802

Lyson's Environs of London, 4 vol[s]., many plates, 1792

Eton's Survey of the Turkish Empire, 1788

Dubois' Description of the People of India, MS notes, 1817

Angeloni's Letters on the English Nation, 2 vol[s]., 1756

Map of North America, by Bowles, in case

Watkin's [Watkinson] Survey of South of Ireland, 1777

Guthrie's System of Modern Geography [no publication date]

Phillippe's Cosmographie Universelle, 77 maps coloured, 1768

Ptolomaei Geographia Universale, 2 tom, Ven., 1598

Lloydii Dictionarium Geograph. et Historia, Lond., 1686

Middleton's System of Geography, 2 vol[s]., plates, 1778

Knolles' Historie of the Turks, heads [?], 1638

Howell's Survey of Venice [1651]

Remarks on the Pictures and Buildings in Rome, 1780

Guides to Modern and Ancient Rome, Dresden, Bologna, Venice, Pozzuoli, Padua, D'Anvers, Florence, Naples, some in French, some Italian, many with plates and of various dates

Appendix 5
Travel Accounts and Printed Materials Related to Geography in Thrale Piozzi's Manuscript Catalogue of Books at Brynbella

8 October 1806
Myddelton's Geography 2 Vols.
Knolly's Turks 1 Vol.
Howell's Venice 1 Vol.
Ptolomy's Geography 1 Vol.
Cook's Voyages 1 Vol.
Book of French Maps 1 Vol.
Herbert's Travels 1 Vol.
Wheler's Travels 1 Vol.
Sandy's Travels 1 Vol.
Lyson's Environs 1 Vol.
Pennant's Snowdonia 1 Vol.
Ansons Voyages
Pennants London 1 Vol.
Anderson's China 1 Vol.
Piozzi's Journey 2 Vols.
Johnson's Hebrides 1 Vol.
Robertson's America 3 Vols.
Krantz's Greenland 2 Vols.
Varenius's Geography 2 Vols.
Byrons Voyages 1 Vol.
Cooke's Voyages 1 Vol.
Harris on the Globes 1 Vol.
Myddelton's Rome 1 Vol.
Lobo's Abyssinia 1 Vol.
D'Anville's Geography 1 Vol.
Coxe's Sketches 1 Vol.

Letters on Poland 1 Vol.
Colden's Canada
Russel's Aleppo
Dickensons Roads
Dutens Roads
Account of Denmark
Harmers Observations 2 Vols.
Gray's Tour 1 Vol.
Hunters Tour 1 Vol.
Smith's Tour 3 Vols.
Vaillants Travels 3 Vols.
Carver's Travels 2 Vols.
Starke's Tour 1 Vol.
Murray's Tour 1 Vol.
Boswell's Tour 1 Vol.
Watkinson's Iceland 1 Vol.
Travels thro' Barbary 2 Vols.
Robertsons America 3 Vols.
Eton on the Turkish Empire 1 Vol.
Acc^t of Verona 2 v
Beauties of Clifton 1
Lady Mary Wortley's Letters 2 Vols.
Voyages de Cyrus 1 Vol.
Voyage de Paris 1 Vol.
Addison's Travels 1 Vol.
Roma antica e Moderna 4 Vols.
Cremona 1 v
Napoli 1
Sir Paul Rycauts Turks
Smollets Travels 2 Vols.
Wilson's Indians 1 Vol
Cooks Voyages 1 Vol.
Roma antica e Moderna
Tour thro' Wales neat pocket Size
Guida de Napoli

Lady M.W. Montagu's 5 Vols.
Helen Maria Williams Letters 2 Vols.
Scotto's Itinerario 1 Vol.
Descrizione di Bologna 1 Vol.
Descrizione di Padua 1 Vol.
Descrizione di Venezia 1 Vol.
Paris H: M: Williams 2 Vols.

Additions made May 1807
Sonnini's Egypt
Browne's Africa

Second Cargo June 1807
Pennants Tours 3 Vols.

Additions Made 1808
Travel Books Africa 2 Vols.
Sample's Travels Spain 2 Vols.

Additions 1813
A[?]ams Geography 1 Vol.

References

Manuscripts Cited

Correspondence, 1743–1826. Mary Hamilton Papers. University of Manchester Library. GB 133 HAM/1.

Dickenson Family of Birch Hall. Preston, Lancashire Archives. DDX 274.

Hester Lynch Piozzi, Catalogue of the Books at Brynbella, 1806–1813. Thrale-Piozzi Manuscripts. University of Manchester Library. GB 133 Eng MS 612

Manuscript Diaries, 1776–1797. Mary Hamilton Papers. University of Manchester Library. GB 133 HAM/2

Printed Primary Sources

'A Catalogue of the Excellent and Genuine Household Furniture . . . Also, the Extensive and Well-Selected Library, Containing near 3000 volumes . . . of Mrs. Piozzi . . . which will be Sold by Auction, by Mr. Squibb, on the Premises, on Wednesday the 8th of May 1816' in *Sale Catalogues of the libraries of Samuel Johnson, Hester Lynch Thrale (Mrs. Piozzi) and James Boswell* (New Castle, DE, 1993), pp. 47–139.

A Catalogue of the Library, Splendid Books of Prints, Poetical and Historical Tracts, of David Garrick, Esq Removed from his Villa at Hampton, and House on the Adelphi Terrace, with the Modern Works Added thereto by Mrs. Garrick, which will be Sold by Auction, by Mr. Sauders at his Great Room, "The Poets' Gallery," No. 39, Fleet Street, on Wednesday, April 23d, 1823 . . .

A Later Pepys: The Correspondence of Sir William Weller Pepys, ed. A.C. C. Gaussen, 2 vols. (London and New York: John Lane, 1904).

A Series of Letters between Mrs. Elizabeth Carter and Miss Catherine Talbot, from the Year 1741 to 1770, 4 vols. (London: F.C. and J. Rivington, 1809).

Aspinall-Oglander, C., *Admiral's Widow: Being the Life and Letters of the Hon. Mrs. Edward Boscawen From 1761 to 1805* (London: The Hogarth Press, 1942).

'Catalogue of the Library, Pictures, Prints, Coins, Plate, China, and other Valuable Curiosities, the Property of Mrs Hester Lynch Piozzi, deceased, to be sold by Auction . . .' in *Sale Catalogues of the libraries of Samuel Johnson, Hester Lynch Thrale (Mrs. Piozzi) and James Boswell* (New Castle, DE, 1993), pp. 141–212.

Crabbe, G., 'The Library' in A.W. Ward (ed.), *Poems by George Crabbe*, vol. 1 (Cambridge: Cambridge University Press, 1905), pp. 100–18.

D'Arblay, M., *Diary and Letters of Madame D'Arblay*, 6 vols. (London: Henry Colburn, 1842–1843).

   Memoirs of Doctor Burney, Arranged From His Own Manuscripts, From Family Papers, and From Personal Recollections, 3 vols. (London: Edward Moxon, 1832).

Gilpin, W., 'An account of the Revd Mr Gilpin, Vicar of Boldre in New Forest, written by himself' in W. Jackson (ed.), *Memoirs of Dr. Richard Gilpin, of Scaleby Castle in Cumberland* (London and Carlisle: B. Quaritch, C. Thurnam, 1879), pp. 109–53.

Letters from Mrs. Elizabeth Carter, to Mrs. Montagu, between the Years 1755 and 1800, 3 vols. (London: F.C. and J. Rivington, 1817).

More, H., '*The Bas Bleu*: or, Conversation' in H. More, *Florio: A Tale, for Fine Gentlemen and Fine Ladies: and, The Bas Bleu; or, Conversation: Two Poems* (London: Cadell, 1786), pp. 65–89.

Pennington, M., *Memoirs of the Life of Mrs. Elizabeth Carter, with a New Edition of Her Poems*, 2 vols. (London: Rivington, 1816).

Piozzi, H.T., *Observations and Reflections made in the Course of a Journey Through France, Italy and Germany* (Ann Arbor: University of Michigan Press; Rexdale: Ambassador Books Limited, 1967).

Roberts, W., *Memoirs of the Life and Correspondence of Mrs. Hannah More*, 2 vols. (New York: Harper & Brothers, 1835).

Seward, [A.], *Elegy on Captain Cook* (London: J. Dodsley, 1780).

The Autobiography and Correspondence of Mary Granville, Mrs. Delany, ed. Lady Llanover, 3 vols. (London: Richard Bentley, 1861–1862).

The Critical Review: or, Annals of Literature. By a Society of Gentlemen, vol. 68 (London: A. Hamilton, 1789).

The European Magazine, and London Review: Containing the Literature, . . . by Philological Society of London, vol. 16 (London: J. Sewell, 1789).

The French Journals of Mrs. Thrale and Dr. Johnson, eds. M. Tyson and H. Guppy (Manchester: The Manchester University Press, 1932).

The Library of Mrs. Elizabeth Vesey 1715–1791 (Newcastle-on-Tyne: William H. Robinson, 1926).

The Piozzi Letters: Correspondence of Hester Lynch Piozzi, 1784–1821 (formerly Mrs. Thrale), ed. E.A. Bloom and L.D. Bloom, 6 vols. (Newark: University of Delaware Press; London and Toronto: Associated University Presses, 1989–2002).

The Posthumous Works of Mrs. Chapone, 2 vols. (London: John Murray and A. Constable, 1807).

Thraliana: The Diary of Mrs. Hester Lynch Thrale (Later Mrs. Piozzi) 1776–1809, ed. K.C. Balderston, 2 vols. (Oxford: Clarendon Press, 1942).

Walpole, H., *The Yale Edition of Horace Walpole's Correspondence*, eds. W. S. Lewis, et al., 48 vols. (New Haven and London: Yale University Press, 1937–1983).

Wraxall, W., *Historical Memoirs of My Own Time*, 2 vols. (London: Cadell and Davies, 1815).

Secondary Works

Barrows, H., 'Introduction' in H.T. Piozzi (ed.), *Observations and Reflections made in the Course of a Journey Through France, Italy and*

Germany (Ann Arbor: University of Michigan Press; Rexdale: Ambassador Books Limited, 1967), pp. vii–xxx.

Batten, C.L., *Pleasurable Instruction: Form and Convention in Eighteenth-Century Travel Literature* (Los Angeles: University of California Press, 1978).

Borm, J., 'Defining Travel: On the Travel Book, Travel Writing and Terminology' in G. Hooper and T. Youngs (eds.), *Perspectives on Travel Writing* (Aldershot: Ashgate, 2004), pp. 13–26.

Brant, C., *Eighteenth-Century Letters and British Culture* (Chippenham and Eastbourne: Palgrave Macmillan, 2010).

Brewer, J., 'Reconstructing the Reader: Prescriptions, Texts and Strategies on Anna Larpent's Reading' in J. Raven, H. Small and N. Tadmor (eds.), *The Practice and Representation of Reading in England* (Cambridge: Cambridge University Press, 1996), pp. 226–45.

Bridges, R., 'Bruce, James (1730–1794): British Traveller' in J. Speake (ed.), *Literature of Travel and Exploration: An Encyclopedia* (London and New York: Routledge, 2013), pp. 130–1.

Buzard, J., 'The Grand Tour and after (1660–1840) in P. Hulme and T. Youngs (eds.), *The Cambridge Companion to Travel Writing* (Cambridge: Cambridge University Press, 2002), pp. 37–52.

Clifford, J.L., *Hester Lynch Piozzi (Mrs. Thrale)*, 2nd ed. (Oxford: Oxford University Press, 1987).

Eger, E., *Bluestockings: Women of Reason from Enlightenment to Romanticism* (Chippenham and Eastbourne: Palgrave Macmillan, 2010).

Ellis, M., 'Reading Practices in Elisabeth Montagu's Epistolary Network of the 1750s' in E. Eger (ed.), *Bluestockings Displayed: Portraiture, Performance and Patronage, 1730–1830* (New York: Cambridge University Press, 2013), pp. 213–32.

Glückler, J., Lazega E. and Hammer I., 'Exploring the Interaction of Space and Networks in the Creation of Knowledge: An Introduction' in

J. Glückler, E. Lazega and I. Hammer (eds.), *Knowledge and Networks* (Springer Open, 2017). DOI:10.1007/978–3-319–45023-0, pp. 1–21.

Heller, D., and S. Heller, 'A Copernican Shift; or, Remapping the Bluestocking Heavens' in D. Heller (ed.), *Bluestockings Now! The Evolution of a Social Role* (Farnham: Ashgate, 2015), pp. 17–54.

Kinsley, Z., *Women Writing the Home Tour, 1682–1812* (Bodmin: Ashgate, 2008).

Miller, D.P., 'Between Hostile Camps: Sir Humphry Davy's Presidency of the Royal Society of London, 1820–1827', *The British Journal for the History of Science*, 16 (1983), 1–47.

Osterhammel, J., *Unfabling the East: The Enlightenment's Encounter with Asia* (Princeton and Oxford: Princeton University Press, 2018).

Outram, D., *The Enlightenment*, 3rd ed. (New York: Cambridge University Press, 2013).

Pelling, M., 'Collecting the World: Female Friendship and Domestic Craft at Bulstrode Park', *Journal for Eighteenth-Century Studies*, 41.1 (2018), 101–20.

Pohl N., and B.A. Schellenberg, 'Introduction: A Bluestocking Historiography' in N. Pohl and B.A. Schellenberg (eds.), *Reconsidering the Bluestockings* (San Marino, CA: Huntington Library, 2003), pp. 1–20.

Schellenberg, B.A., 'Bluestocking Women and the Negotiation of Oral, Manuscript, and Print Cultures' in J.M. Labbe (ed.), *The History of British Women's Writing, 1750–1830* (Chippenham and Eastbourne: Palgrave Macmillan, 2019), pp. 63–83.

'Reading in an Epistolary Community in Eighteenth-Century England' in D.R. Sedo (ed.), *Reading Communities from Salons to Cyberspace* (Chippenham and Eastbourne: Palgrave Macmillan, 2011), pp. 25–43.

Secord, J.A., 'How Scientific Conversation Became Shop Talk', *Transactions of the Royal Historical Society*, Sixth Series, 17 (2007), 129–56.

Stefanelli, M.A., 'Elizabeth Vesey and the Art of Educating Oneself, Between London and Lucan', *Studi Irlandesi: A Journal of Irish Studies*, 3 (2013), 323–34.

Thell, A.M., *Minds in Motion: Imagining Empiricism in Eighteenth-Century British Travel Literature* (Lewisburg: Bucknell University Press, 2017).

Thompson, C., *Travel Writing* (London and New York: Routledge, 2011).
'Journeys to Authority: Reassessing Women's Early Travel Writing, 1763–1862', *Women's Writing*, 24.2 (2017), 131–50, DOI: 10.1080/ 09699082.2016.1207915.

Tobin, B.F., 'Bluestockings and the Cultures of Natural History' in D. Heller (ed.), *Bluestockings Now! The Evolution of a Social Role* (Farnham: Ashgate, 2015), pp. 55–69.

Towsey, M., 'First Steps in Associational Reading: Book Use and Sociability at the Wigtown Subscription Library, 1795–9', *The Papers of the Bibliographical Society of America*, 104.3 (2009), 455–95.
' "I can't resist sending you the book": Private Libraries, Elite Women, and Shared Reading Practices in Georgian Britain', *Library & Information History*, 29.3 (2013), 210–22.
'Women as Readers and Writers' in C. Ingrassia (ed.), *The Cambridge Companion to Women's Writing in Britain, 1660–1789* (Cambridge: Cambridge University Press, 2015), pp. 21–36.

Turner, K., *British Travel Writers in Europe 1750–1800: Authorship, Gender and National Identity* (Aldershot and Burlington: Ashgate, 2001).

Tyson, M., and H. Guppy, 'Introduction' in M. Tyson and H. Guppy (eds.), *The French Journals of Mrs. Thrale and Dr. Johnson* (Manchester: The Manchester University Press, 1932), pp. 1–66.

Voloshkova, N., ' "My friend Mr. H. Walpole": Mary Hamilton, Horace Walpole and the Art of Conversation', *Image [&] Narrative*, 18.3 (2017), 94–106. Accessed at www.imageandnarrative.be/index.php /imagenarrative/article/view/1600/1261

'The Dutiful Daughter: Mary Hamilton's Journal of her Visit to Spa in 1776' in P.J. Corfield and L. Hannan (eds.), *Hats off, Gentlemen! Changing Arts of Communication in the Eighteenth Century* (Paris: Honoré Champion Éditeur, 2017), pp. 89–108.

Williams, A., *The Social Life of Books: Reading Together in the Eighteenth-Century Home* (New Haven and London: Yale University Press, 2017).

Cambridge Elements ☰

Publishing and Book Culture

SERIES EDITOR
Samantha Rayner
University College London

Samantha Rayner is a Reader in UCL's Department of Information Studies. She is also Director of UCL's Centre for Publishing, co-Director of the Bloomsbury CHAPTER (Communication History, Authorship, Publishing, Textual Editing and Reading) and co-editor of the Academic Book of the Future BOOC (Book as Open Online Content) with UCL Press.

ASSOCIATE EDITOR
Leah Tether
University of Bristol

Leah Tether is Professor of Medieval Literature and Publishing at the University of Bristol. With an academic background in medieval French and English literature and a professional background in trade publishing, Leah has combined her expertise and developed an international research profile in book and publishing history from manuscript to digital.

ABOUT THE SERIES

This series aims to fill the demand for easily accessible, quality texts available for teaching and research in the diverse and dynamic fields of Publishing and Book Culture. Rigorously researched and peer-reviewed Elements will be published under themes, or 'Gatherings'. These Elements should be the first check point for researchers or students working on that area of publishing and book trade history and practice: we hope that, situated so logically at Cambridge University Press, where academic publishing in the UK began, it will develop to create an unrivalled space where these histories and practices can be investigated and preserved.

Cambridge Elements ☰

Publishing and Book Culture

Women, Publishing, and Book Culture

Gathering Editor: Rebecca Lyons

Rebecca Lyons is a Teaching Fellow at the University of
Bristol. She is also co-editor of the experimental BOOC (Book
as Open Online Content) at UCL Press. She teaches and
researches book and reading history, particularly female
owners and readers of Arthurian literature in fifteenth- and
sixteenth-century England, and also has research interests in
digital academic publishing.